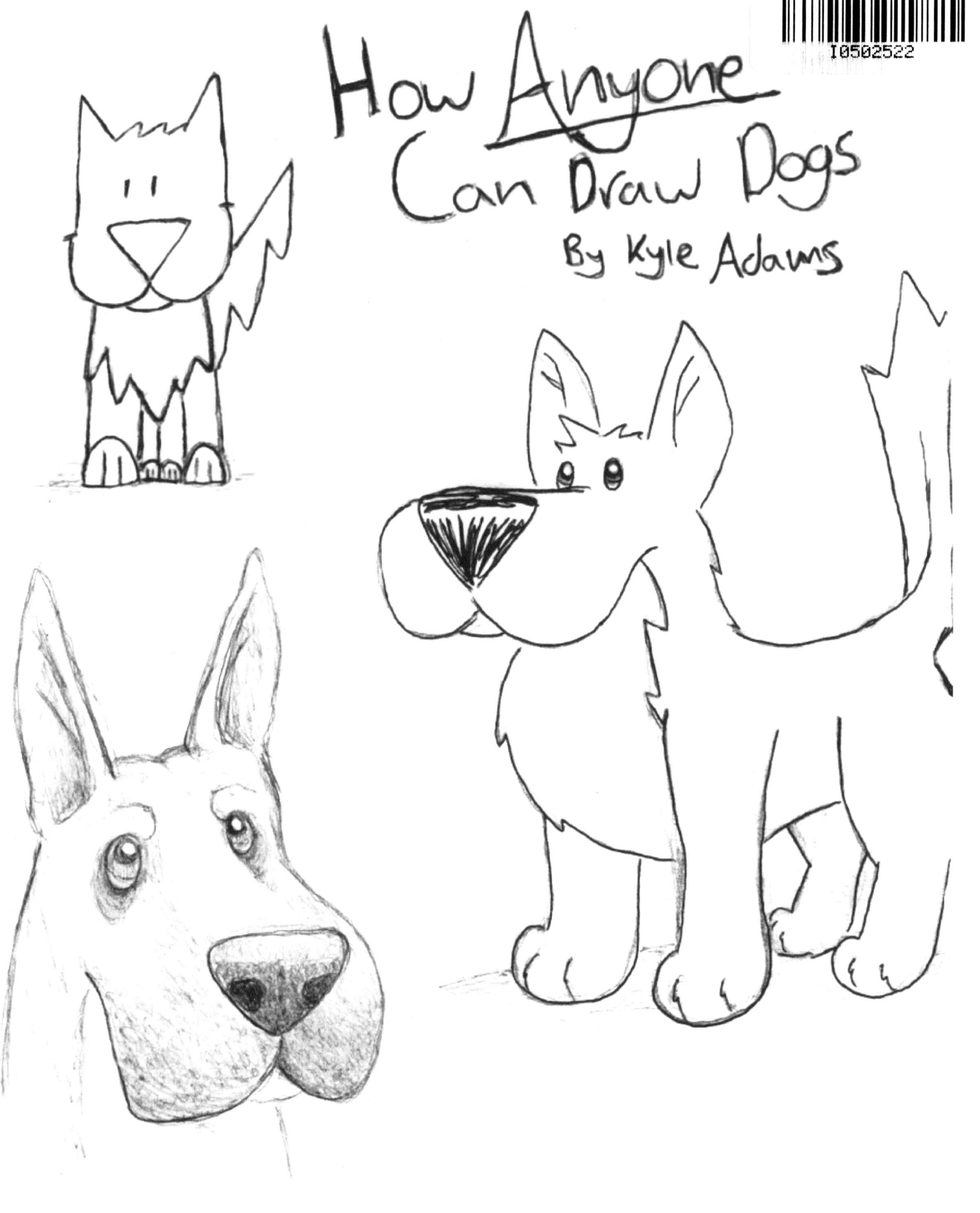

# How Anyone Can Draw Dogs

### By Kyle Adams

I dedicate this book to my brother Zack
and all the fun times we had together growing up.
I would not be the artist I am today were it not for you.

# Attention!

First thing, before doing anything, on a blank piece of paper draw a dog to the best of your ability without using any references. Put this drawing with all of the other drawings you are going to do in a safe place. I recommend having a notebook, sketch book, or folder specifically for the drawings you are going to do in this book. When you have completed all of the activities it will be fun for you to look back and see how far you have come.

# Phase 1
# Start Simple

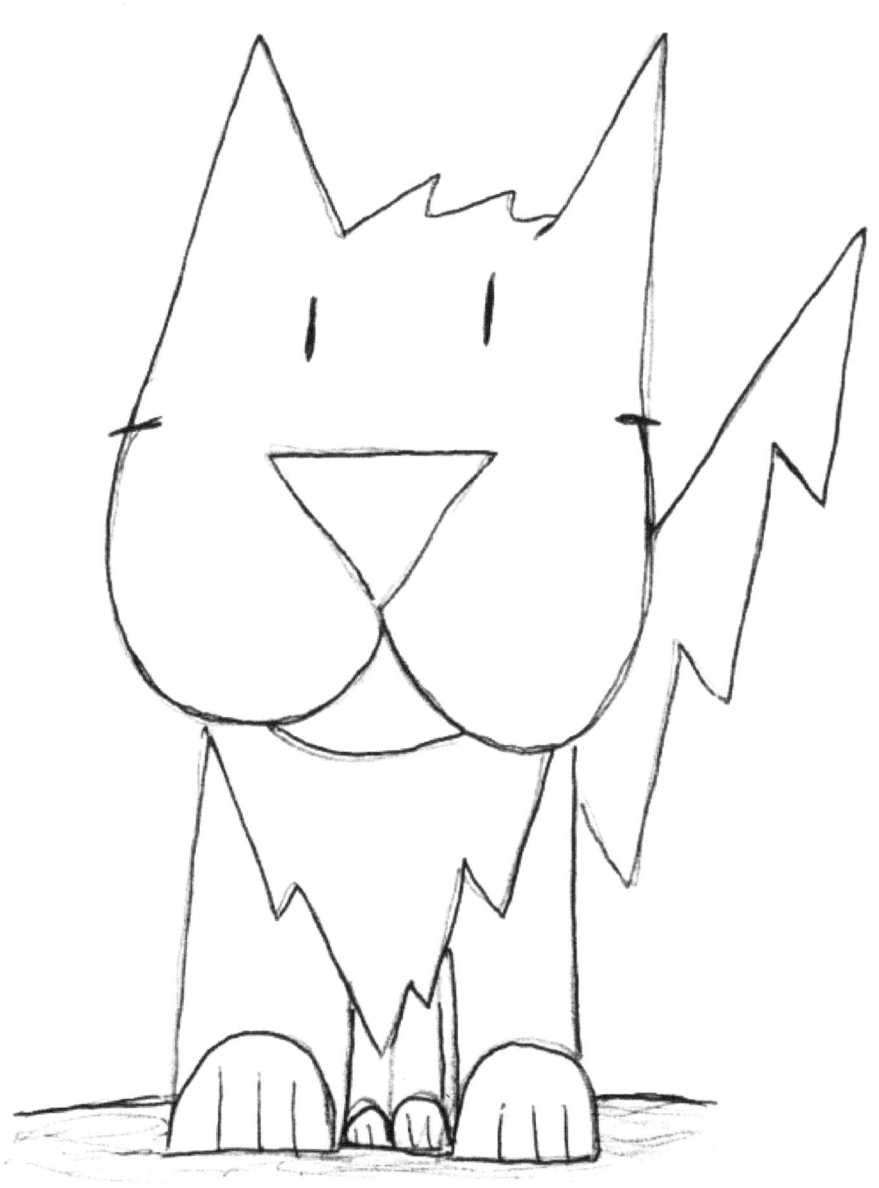

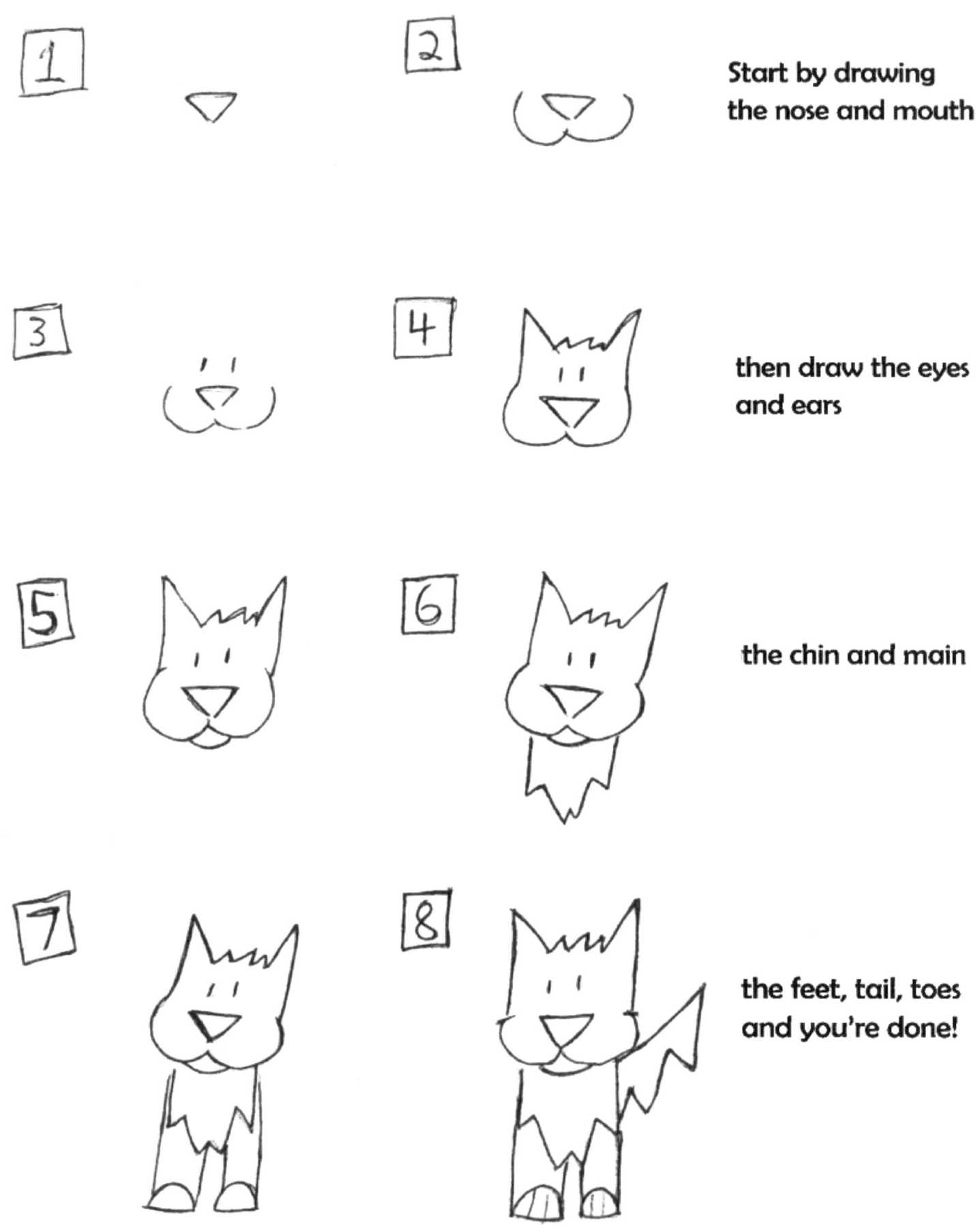

**1**

**2** Start by drawing the nose and mouth

**3**

**4** then draw the eyes and ears

**5**

**6** the chin and main

**7**

**8** the feet, tail, toes and you're done!

**Really simple, right?**
**Don't move on yet though,**
**practice that first until**
**you have it memorized and**
**can draw that without using**
**any references (meaning this**
**book or any of your other**
**drawings).**

Now that you have that memorized, experiment with it and try changing it around.

For some examples:
Try drawing the eyes in different ways

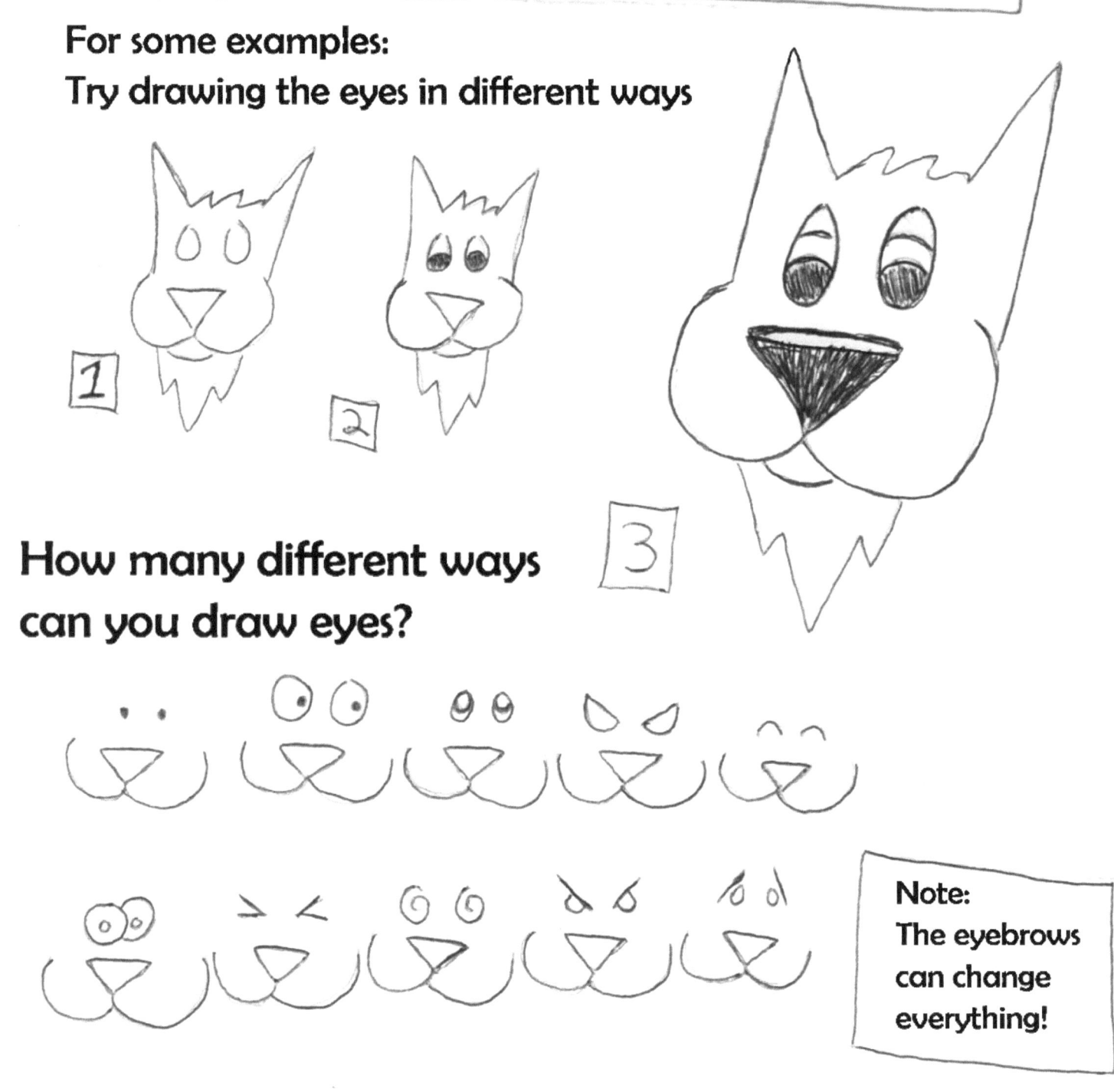

How many different ways can you draw eyes?

Note:
The eyebrows can change everything!

There are tons of different ways to draw eyes. Look around at how different artists draw eyes, and once again experiment. The best way to learn is by experimenting. Try and come up with your own ways of drawing eyes.

# Different Ears

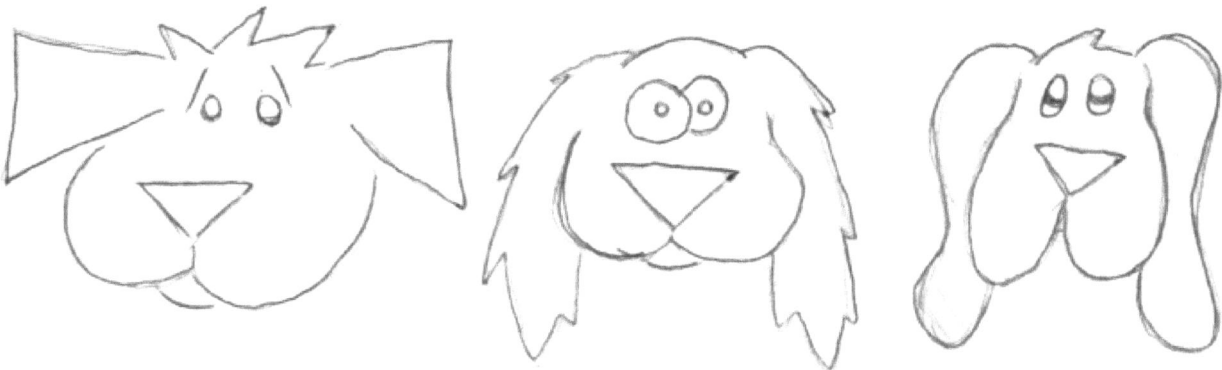

## How to make the tongue hang out

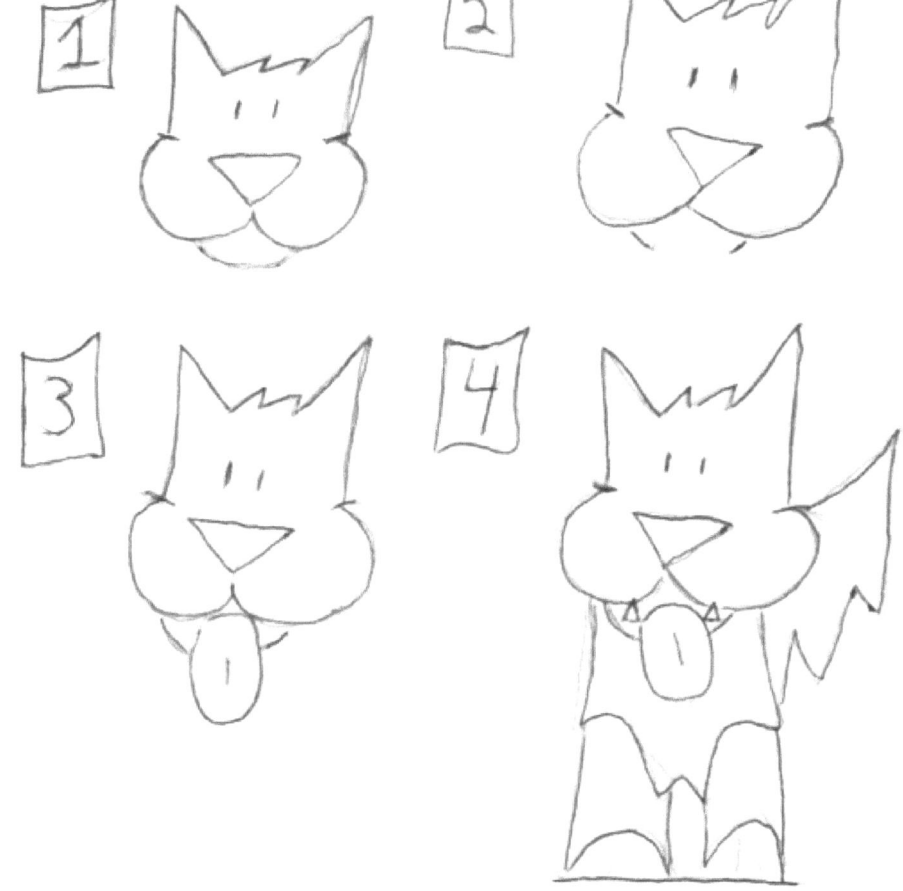

Make sure when you lightly draw the chin, that you make it bigger than normal.

# Different Positions

## The Back end Showing

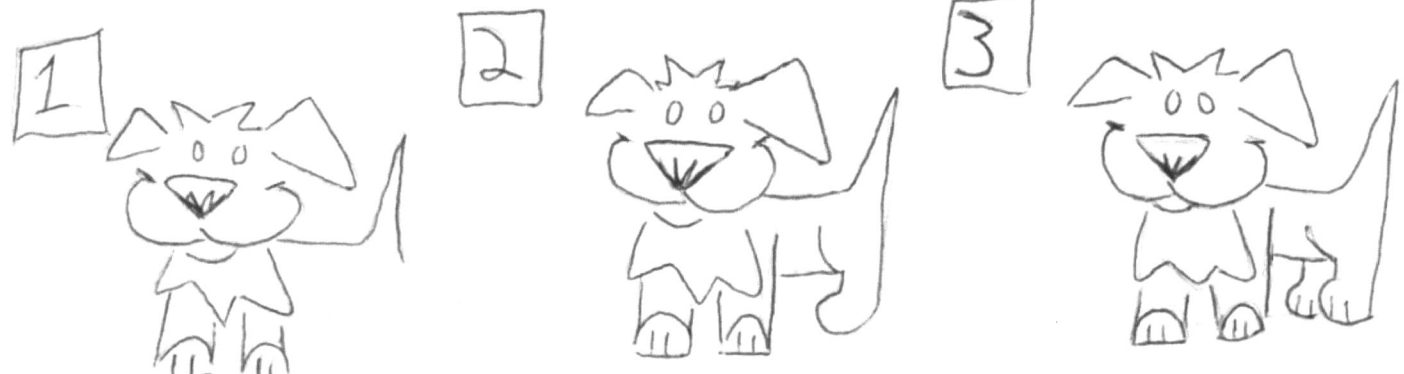

## The Sideways Position

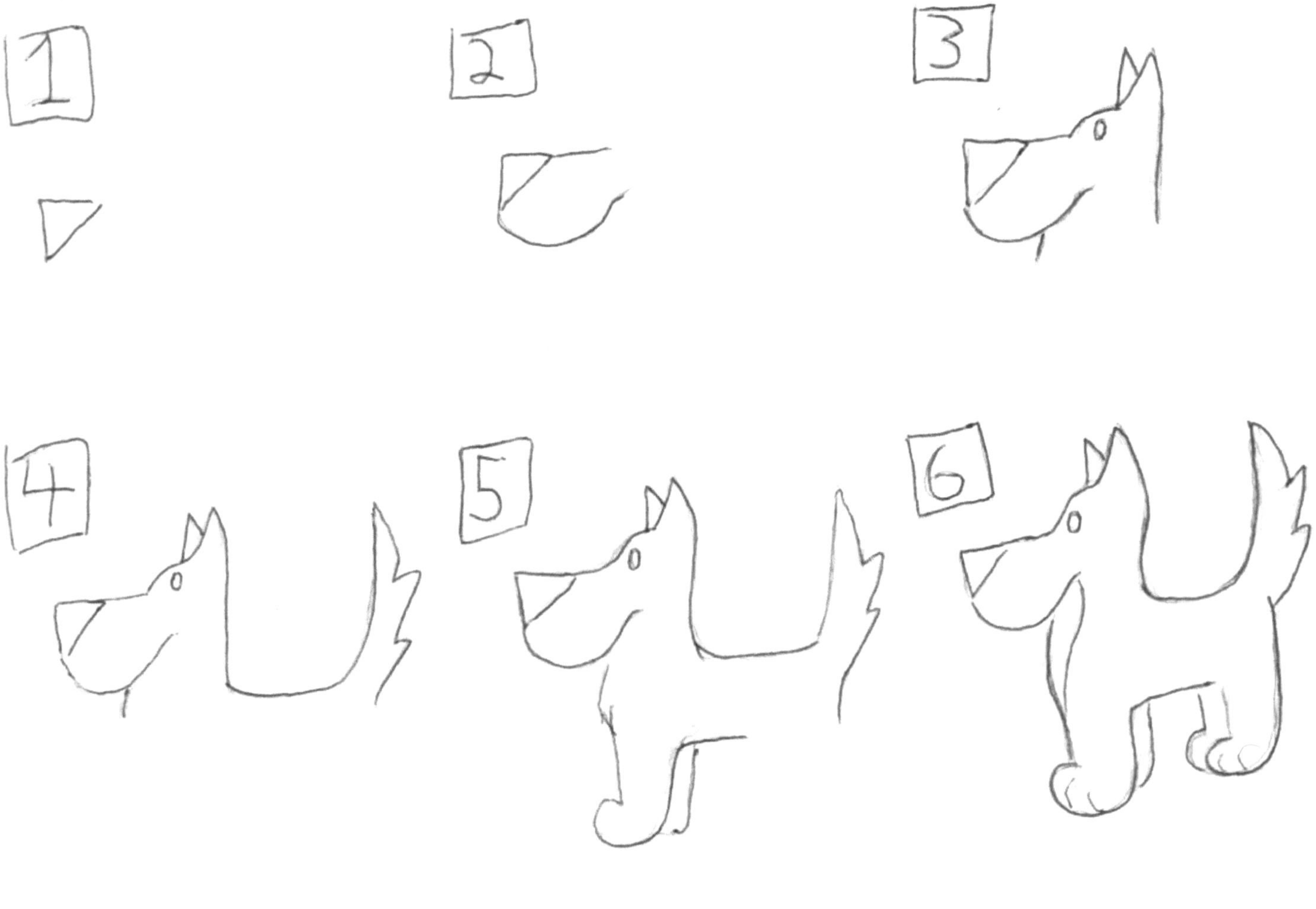

1

2

3

4

5

6

**O**kay, before going on experiment, have fun, do some mix and matching, try coloring your pictures, and go show your drawings to your friends and family.

A few examples of some experiments would be...

- Try drawing a dog with a really long tongue
- Try drawing a dog with one floppy ear and the other ear pointy.
- Try drawing a dog with a bone, stick, ball, or chew toy in its mouth.
- Try drawing a bunch of dogs playing your favorite sport.
-Try drawing a dog that is fighting some kind of monster. (My favorite is dogs fighting dragons.)

Remember, it is really hard to learn how to draw dogs well if you don't decide to have fun with it.

Here are some examples of some drawings that I have done in the past, when I was in this phase of drawing.

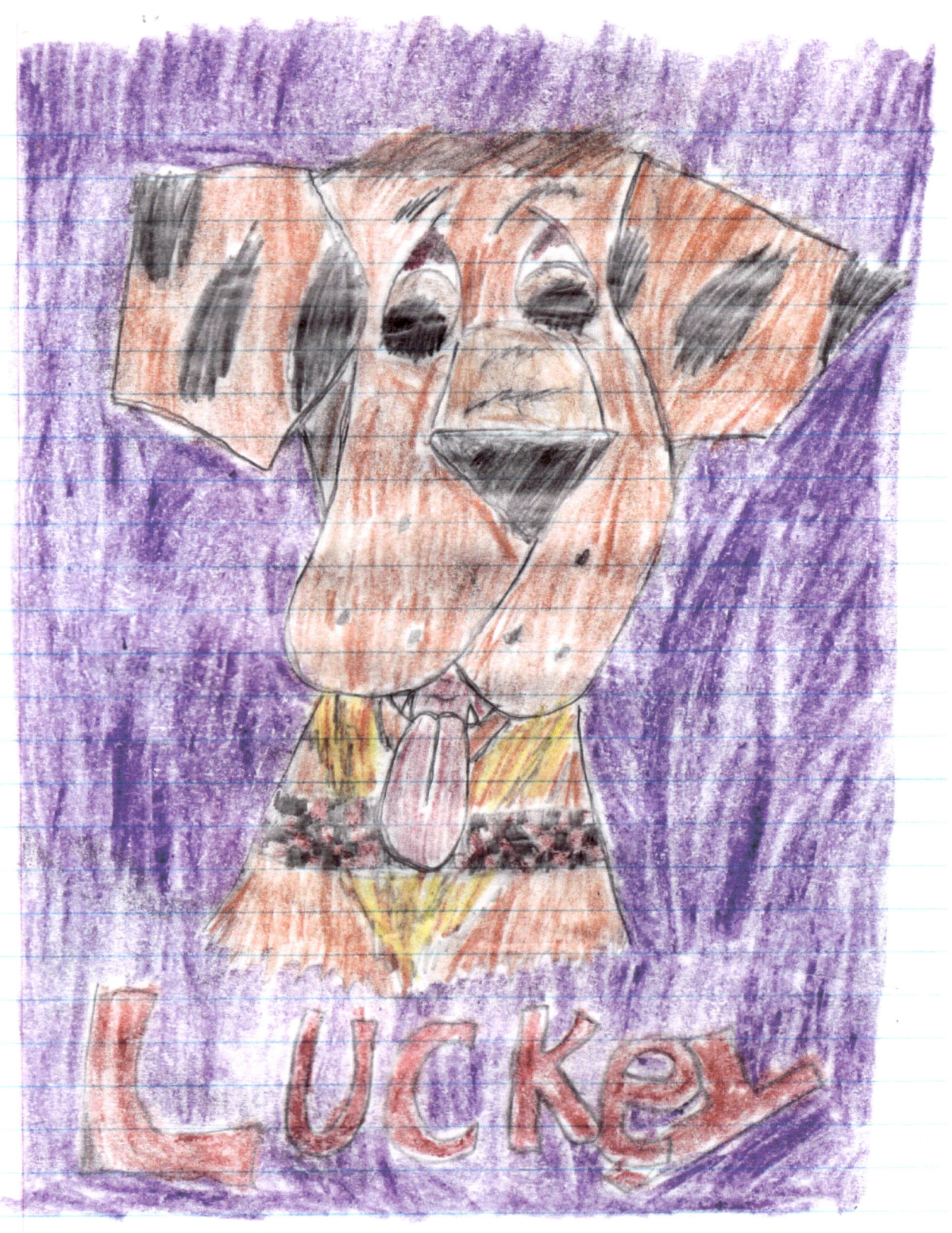

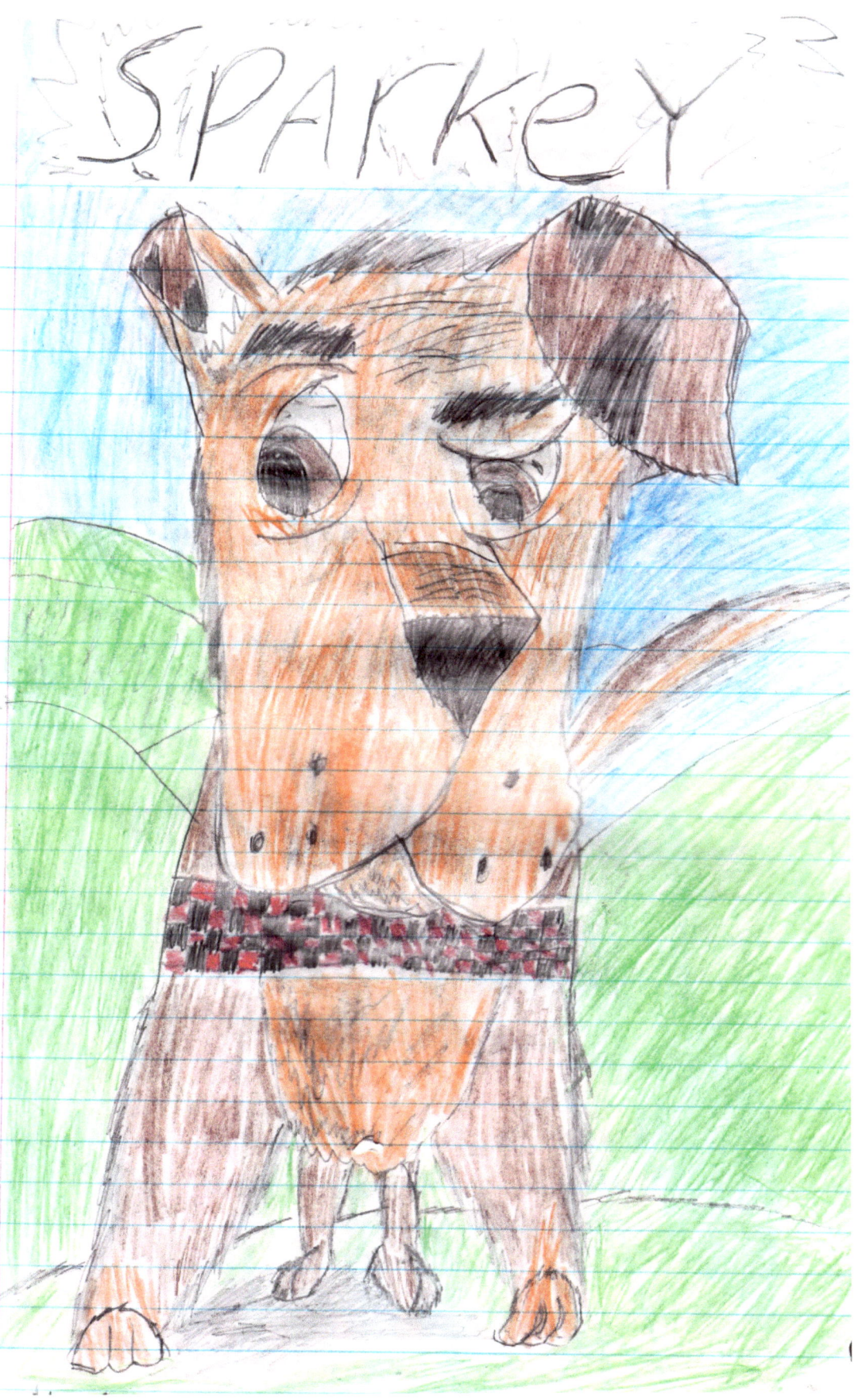

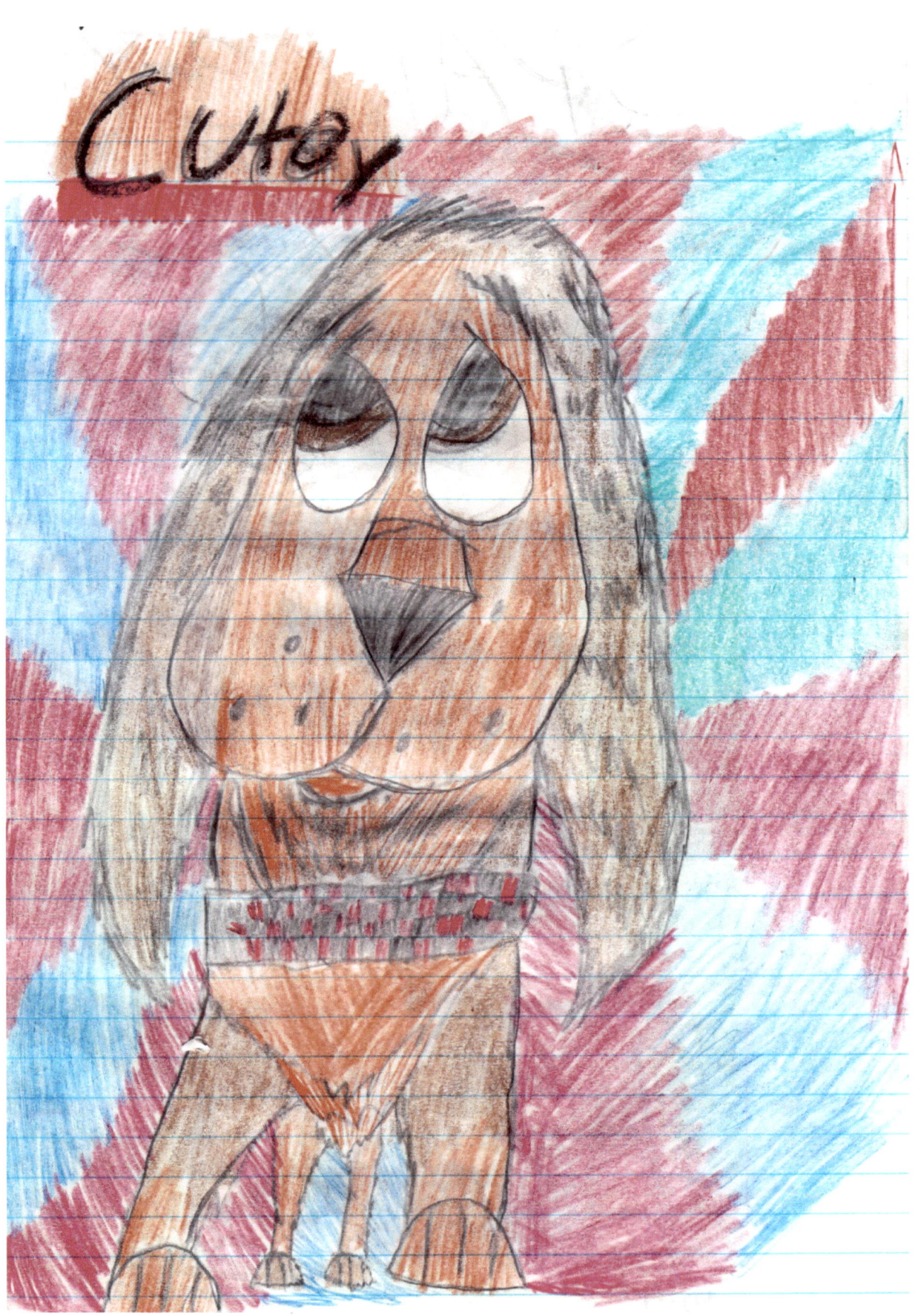

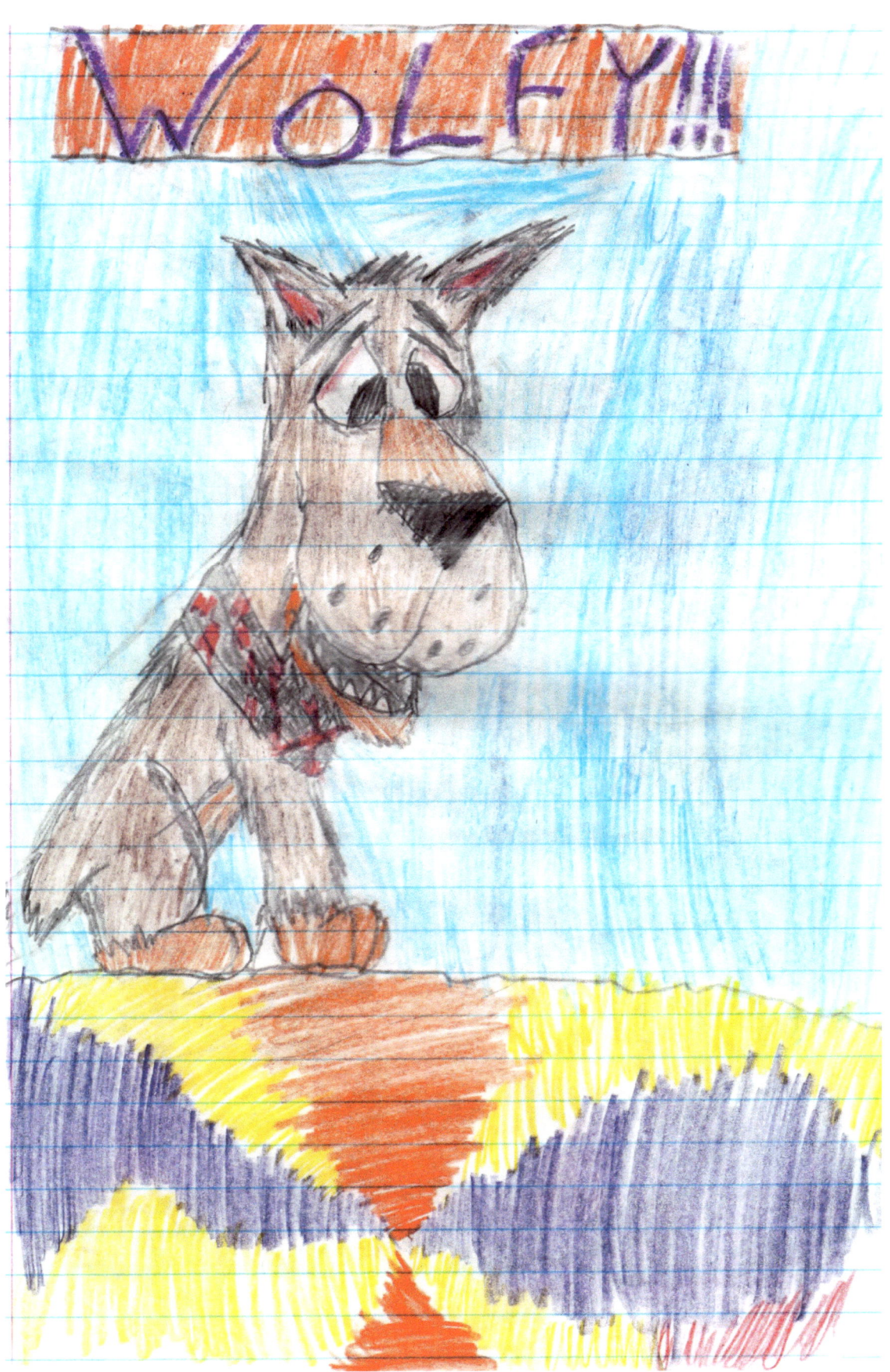

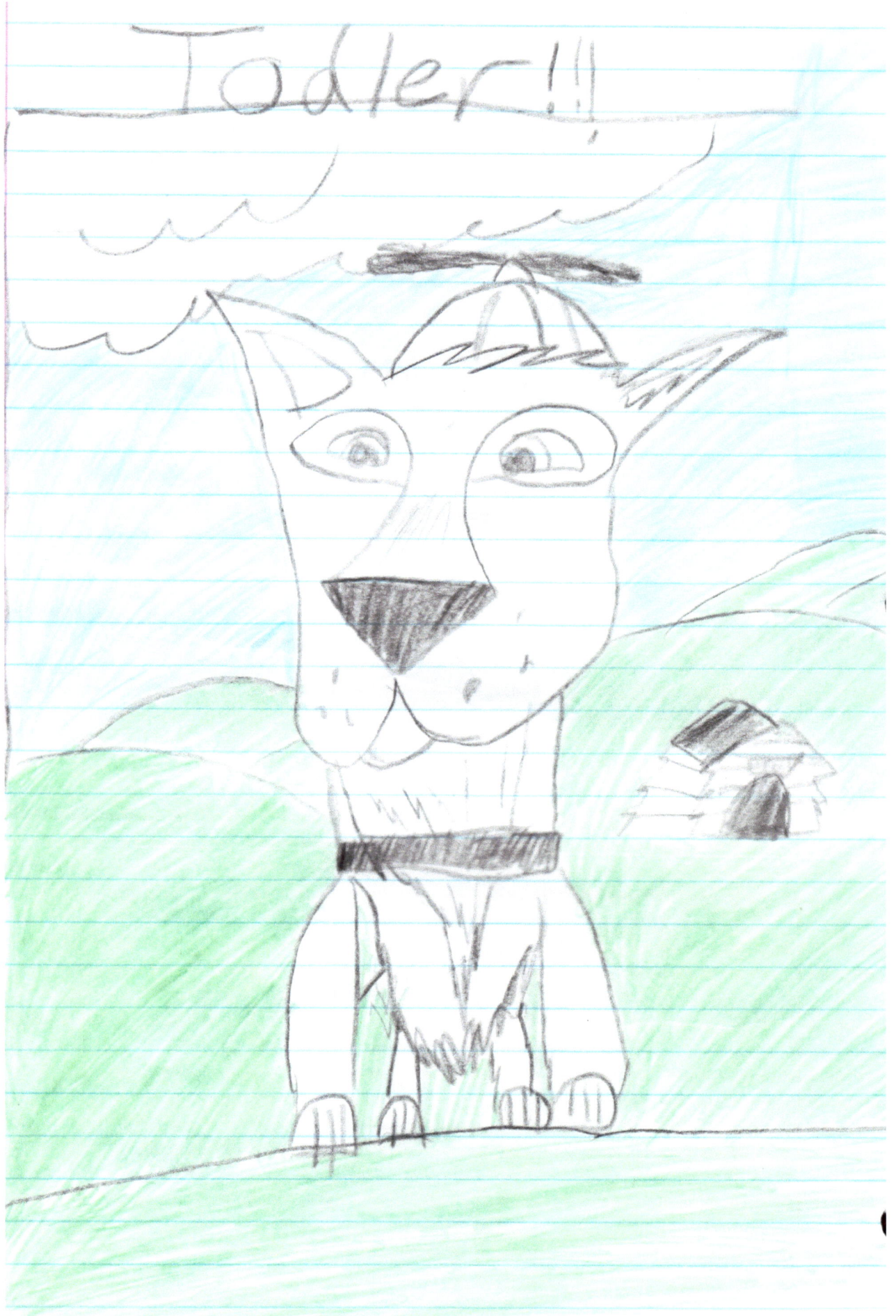

Before moving on to Phase 2,
go back and practice drawing
The phase 1 dog a little more,
drawing it step by step. When
you feel confident with the
Phase 1 dog and can draw it
without references, move
on to phase 2.

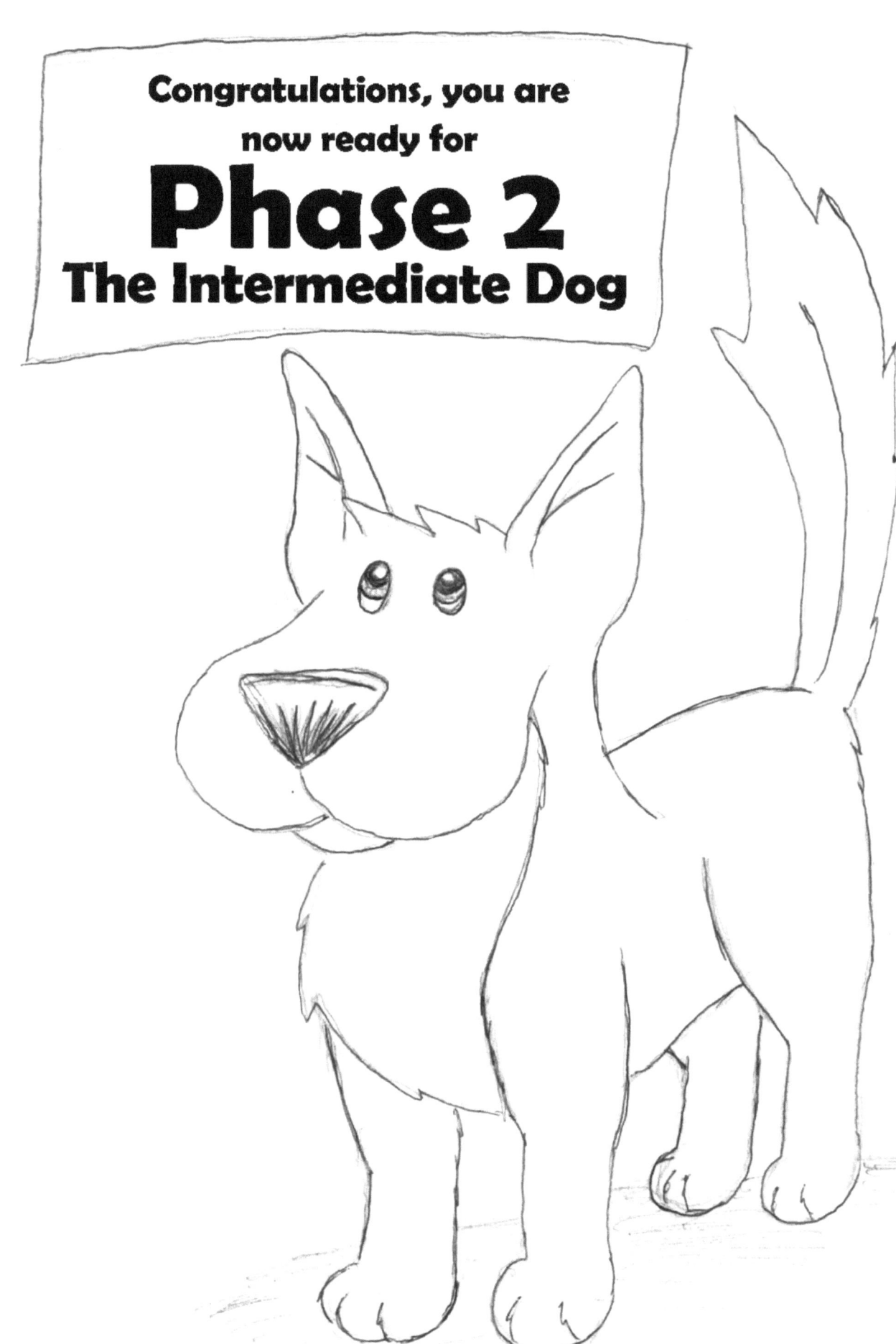

# The Intermediate Dog

You will notice that most of the steps in drawing the Phase 2 Dog are almost exactly the same as the steps in drawing the Phase 1 Dog. There are mostly just little differences, but like the eyebrows, little differences can make big differences.

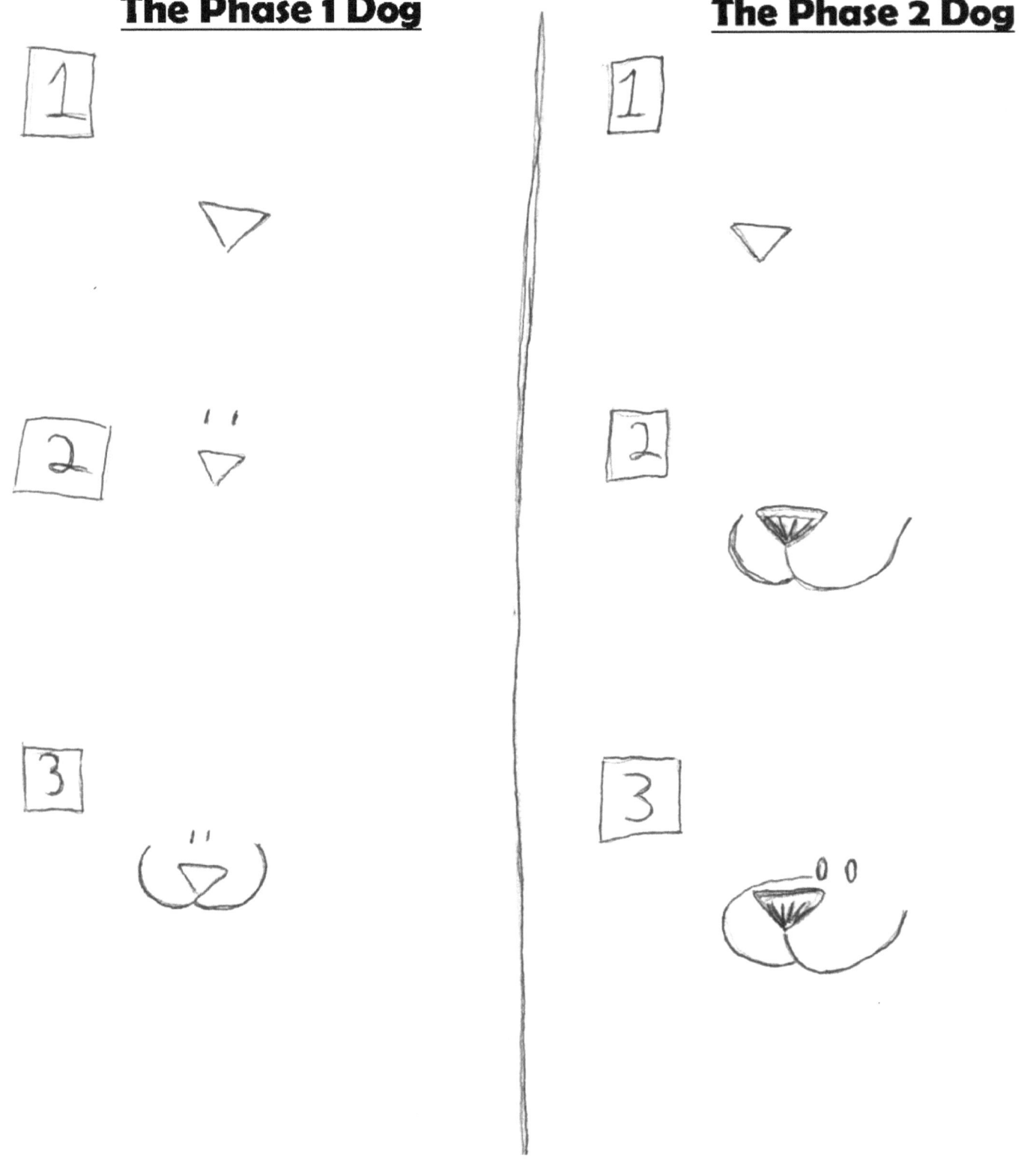

**The Phase 1 Dog**

**The Phase 2 Dog**

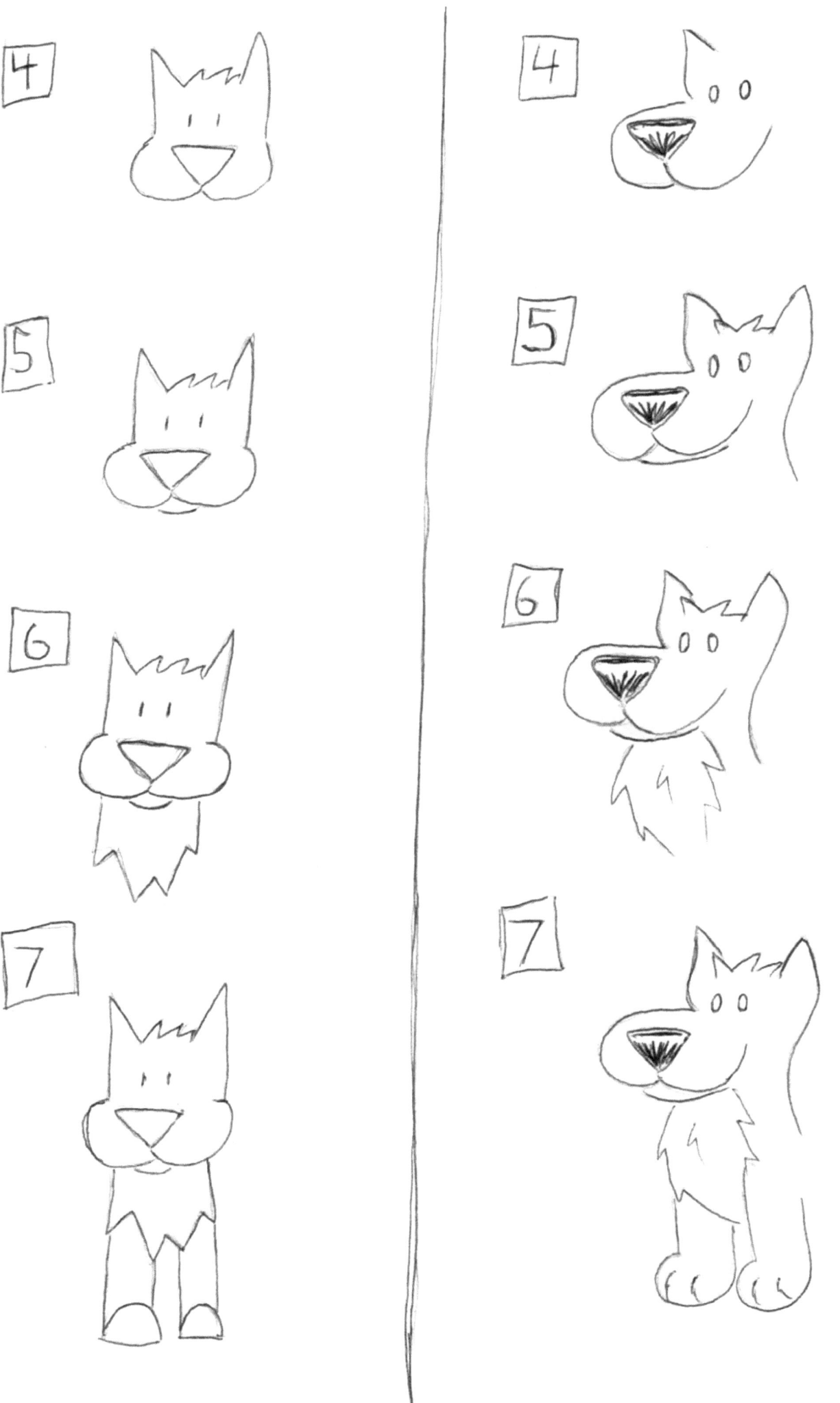

8

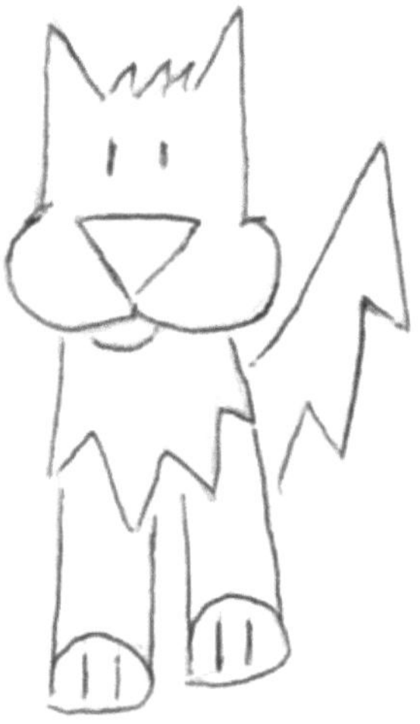

**With Back end Showing**

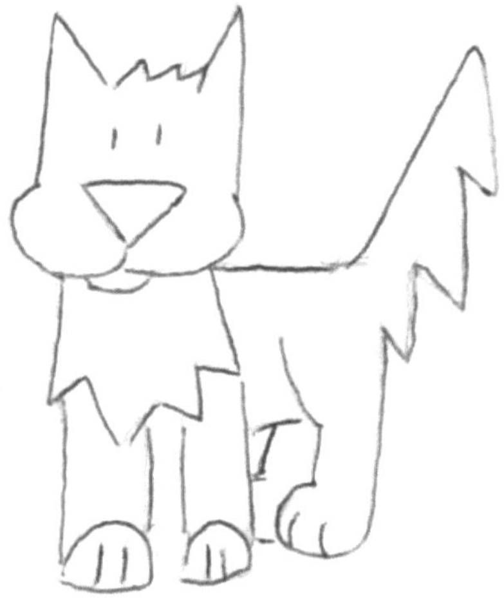

8

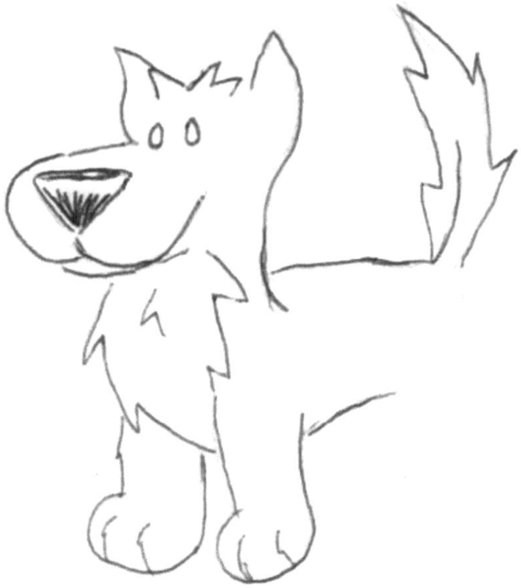

9

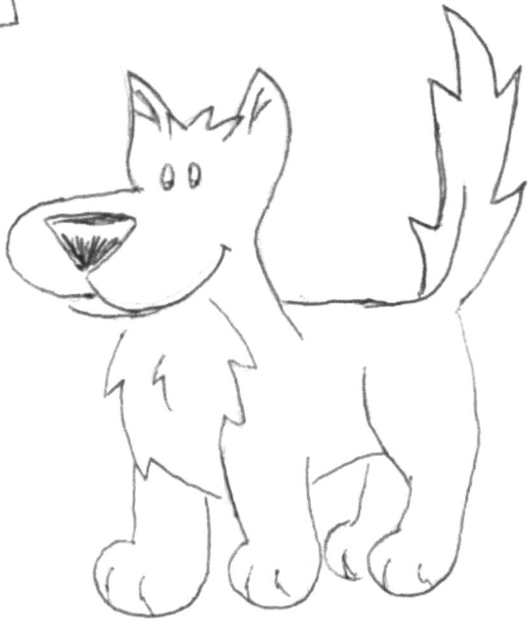

When you have that down try drawing it in the opposite direction.

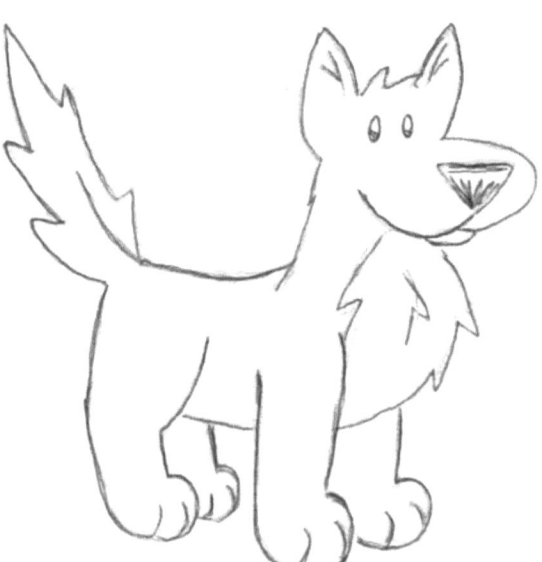

# A few little adjustments  really do go a long way.

Don't expect to draw the Phase 2 Dog perfect after your first try,
it takes practice. It took me years to teach myself what I am teaching
you in a matter of moments.

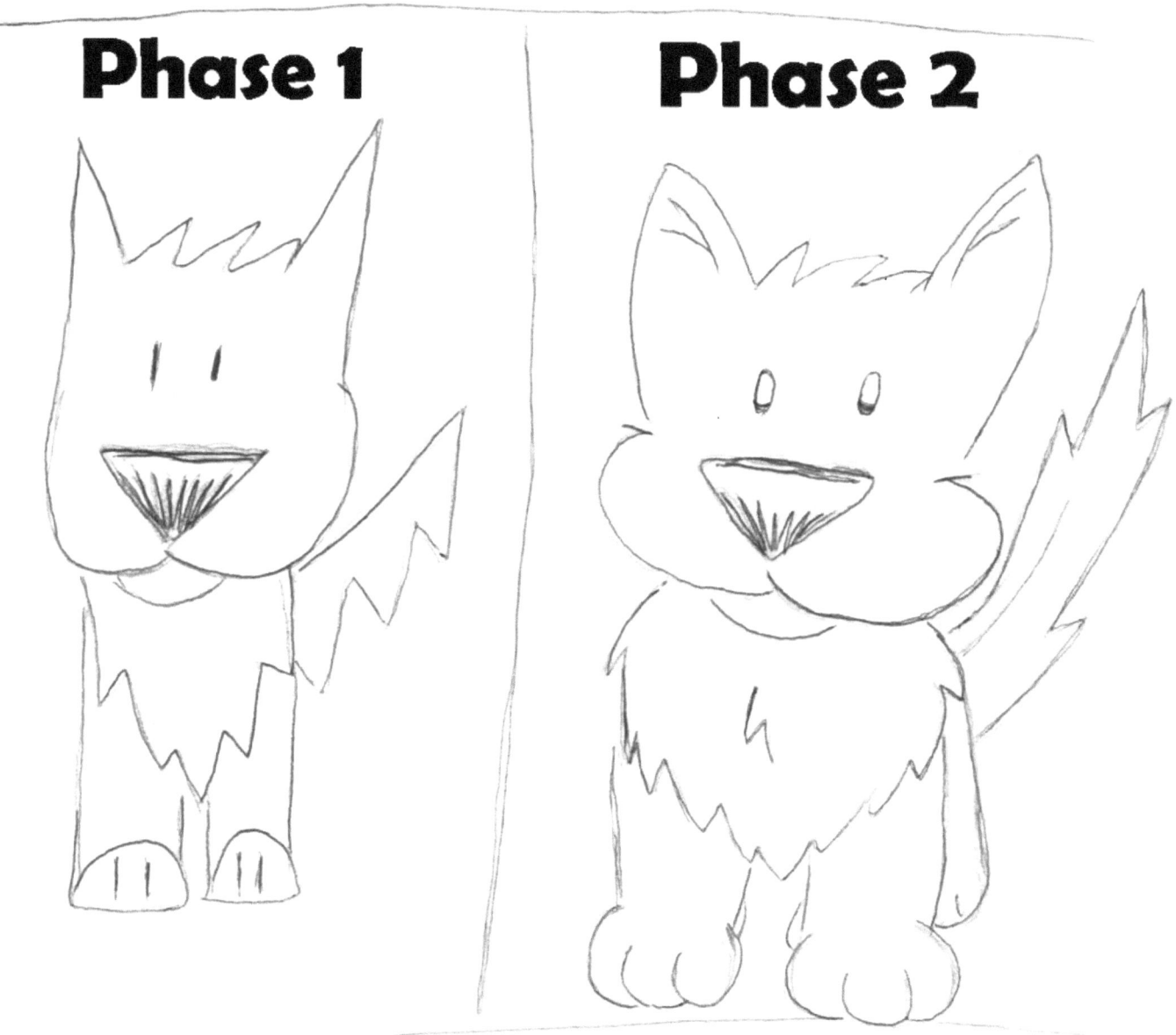

**Phase 1**

**Phase 2**

What will help you most will be focusing on how you draw
the ears, nose, mane, feet, and tail. When you feel confident
in drawing that, move on.

# The Open Mouth

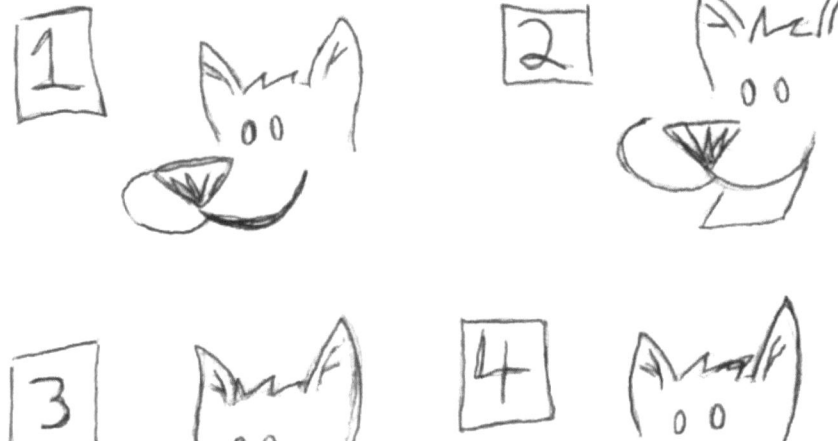

Draw step 2
lightly, it may
take you a few tries
to get it to where
you want it.

# Sitting Down

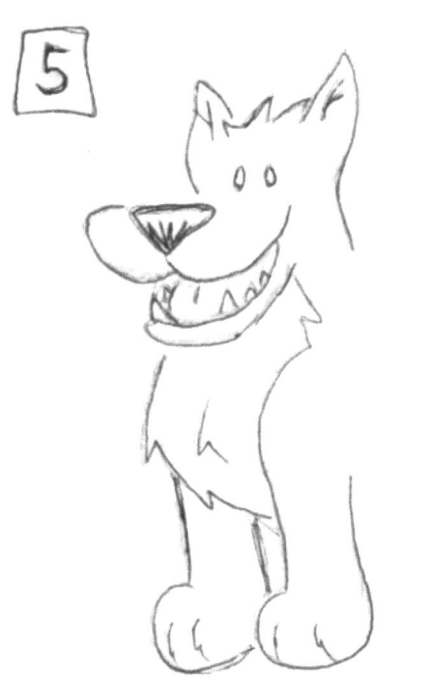

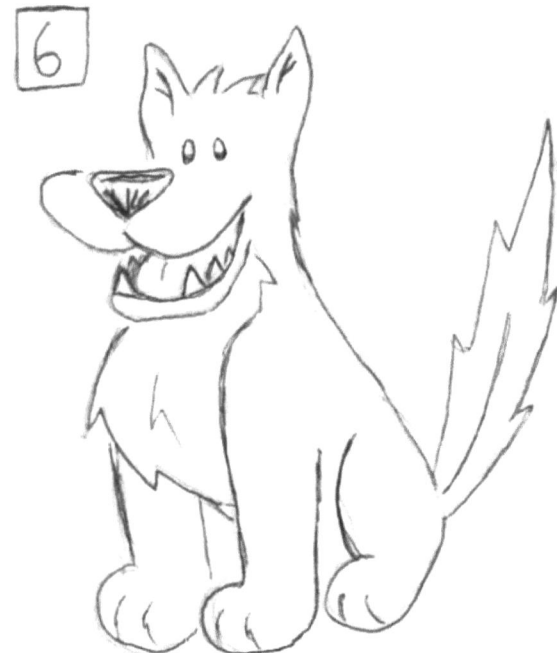

# The Eye of Intensity
- I recommend using this on large drawings -

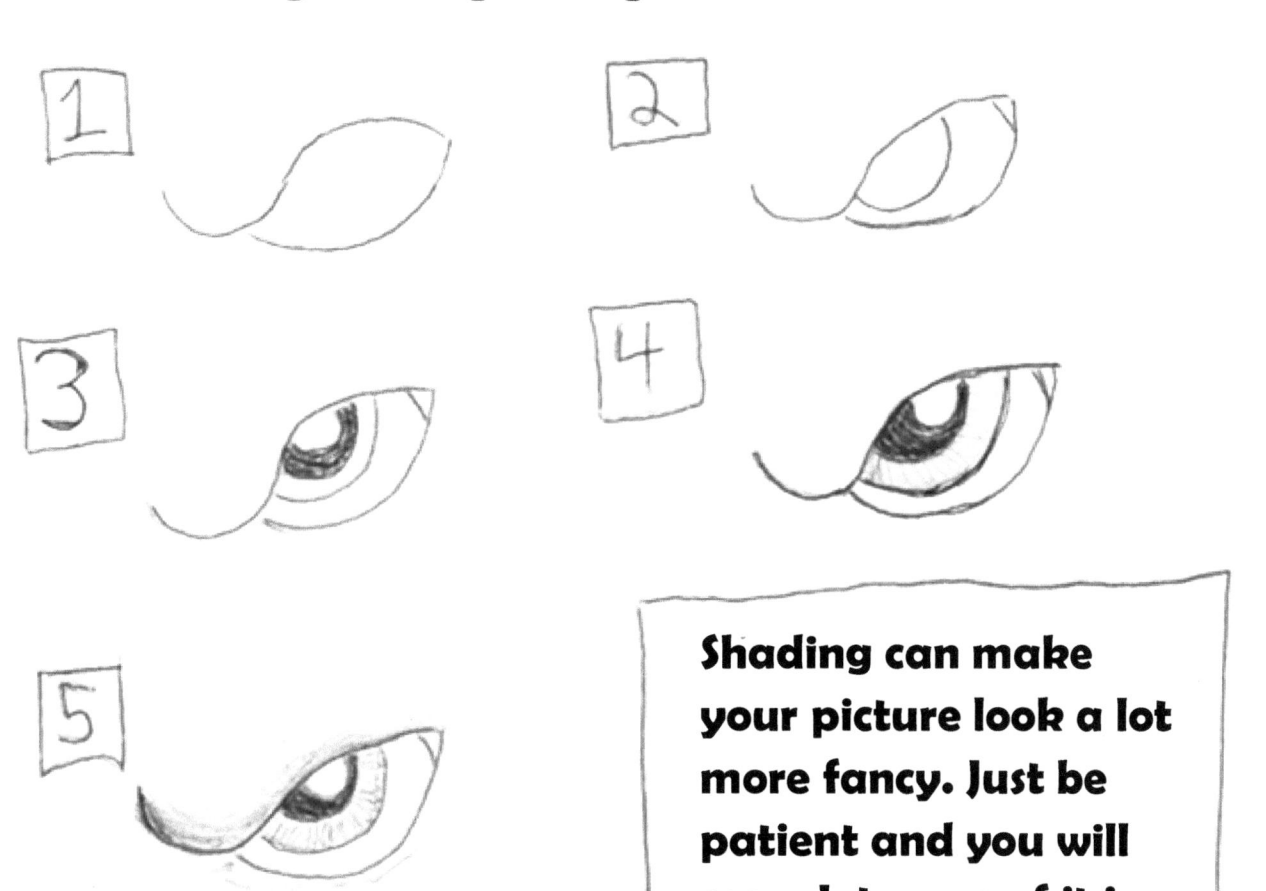

Shading can make your picture look a lot more fancy. Just be patient and you will see a lot more of it in Phase 3.

# Growling

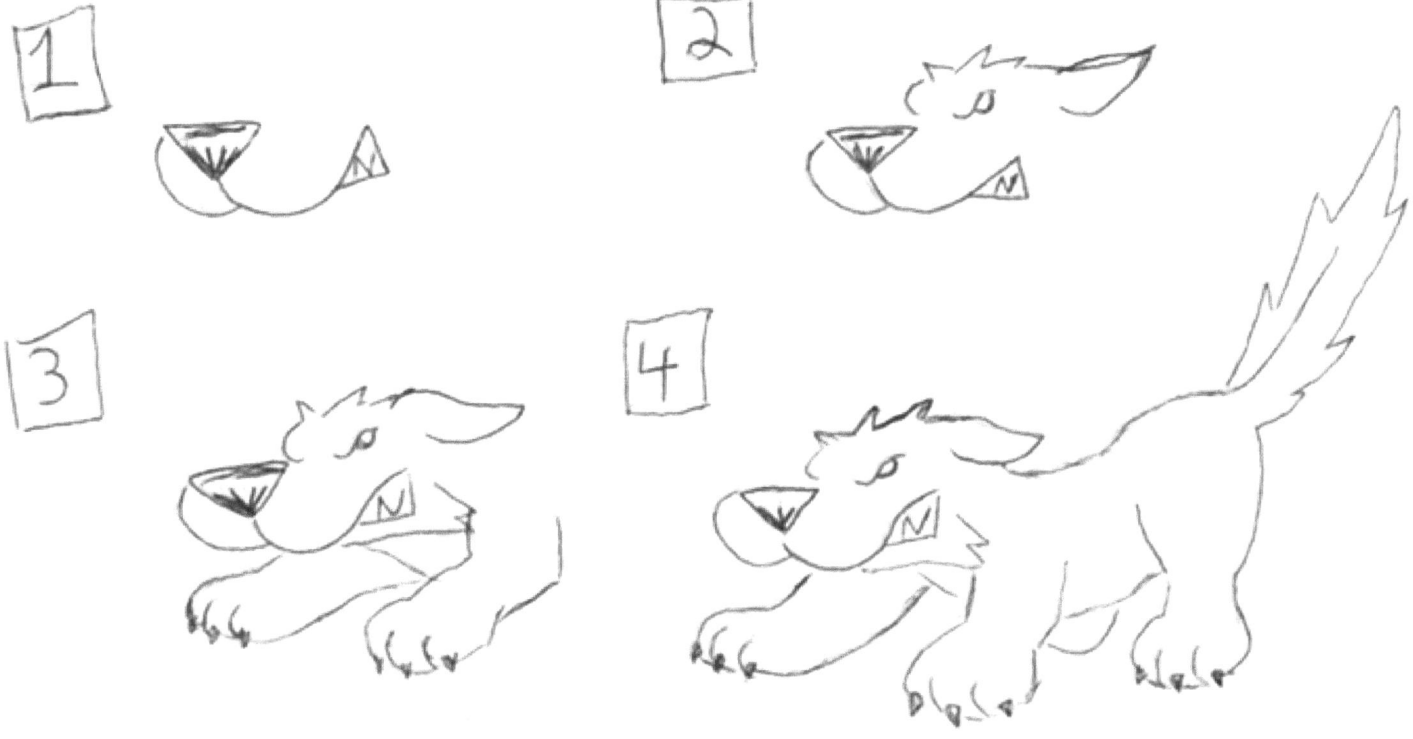

# Skeletons

Sometimes when I am trying to draw a dog in an unusual position it can be easier when I draw a light skeleton/ stick figure first. After I get the positioning right, I then add the rest of the body.

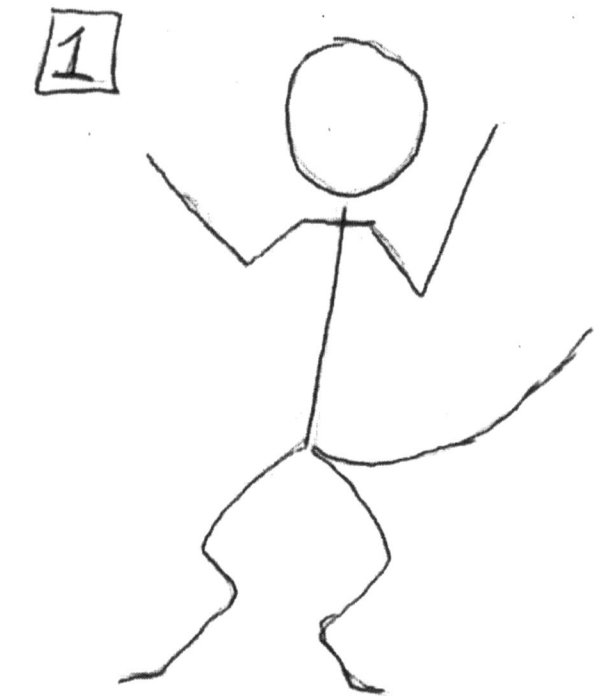

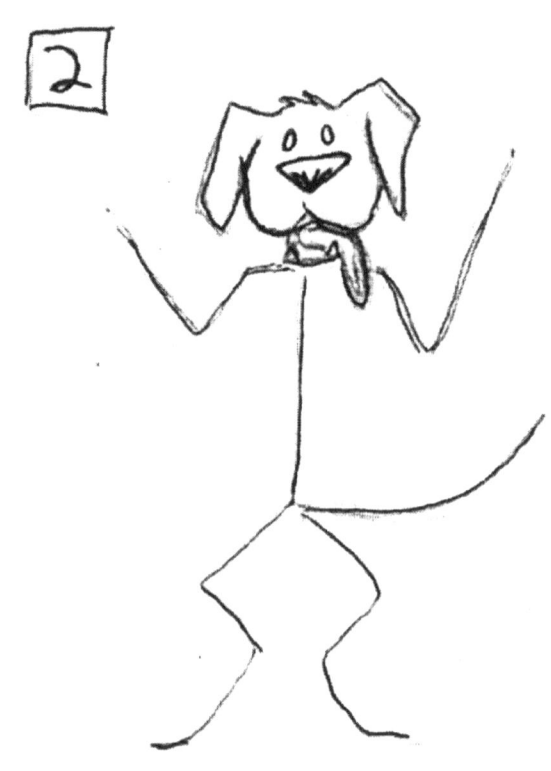

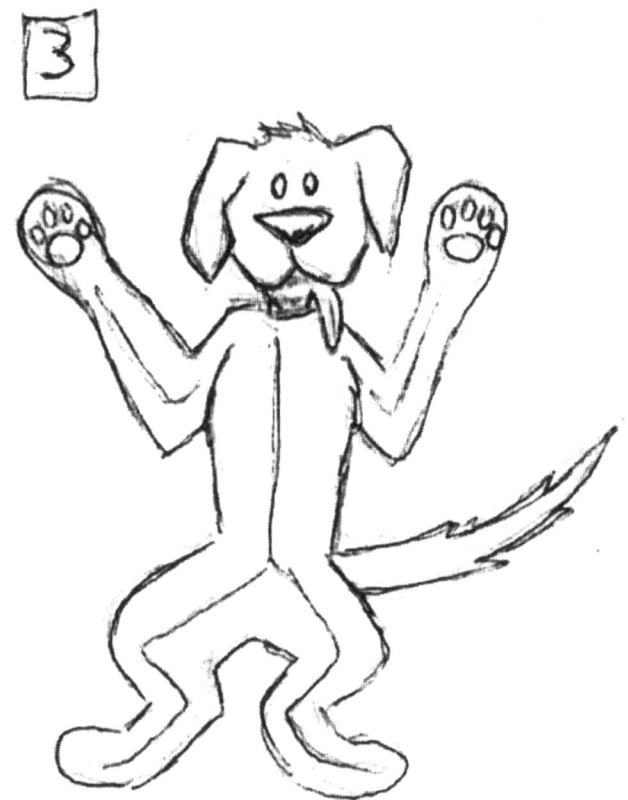

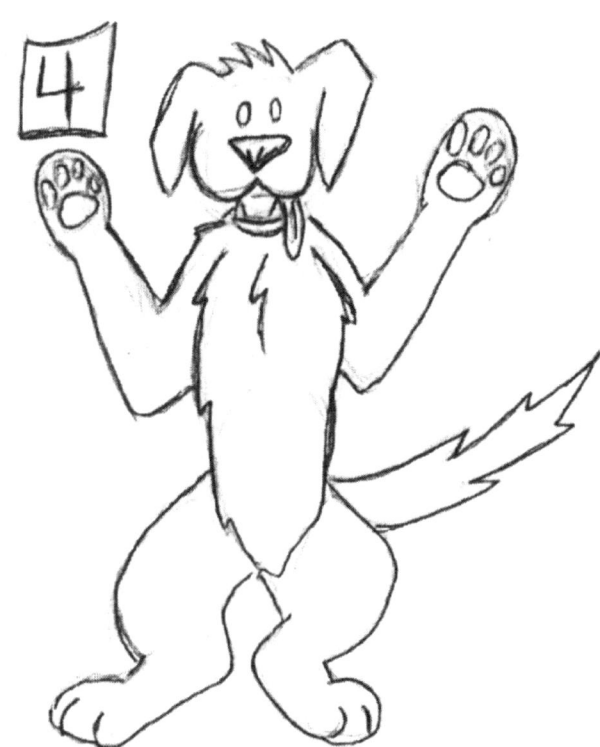

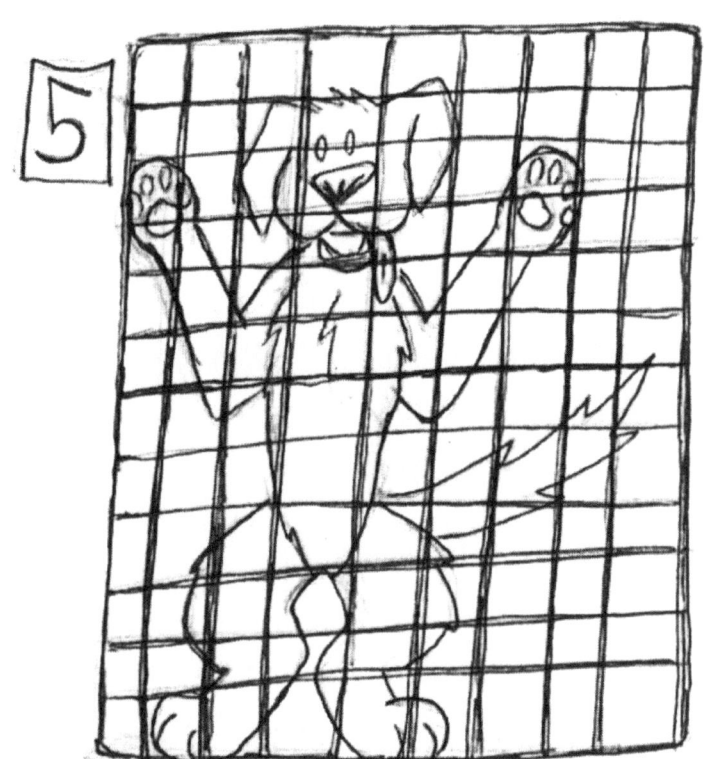

## Dog Playing Basketball

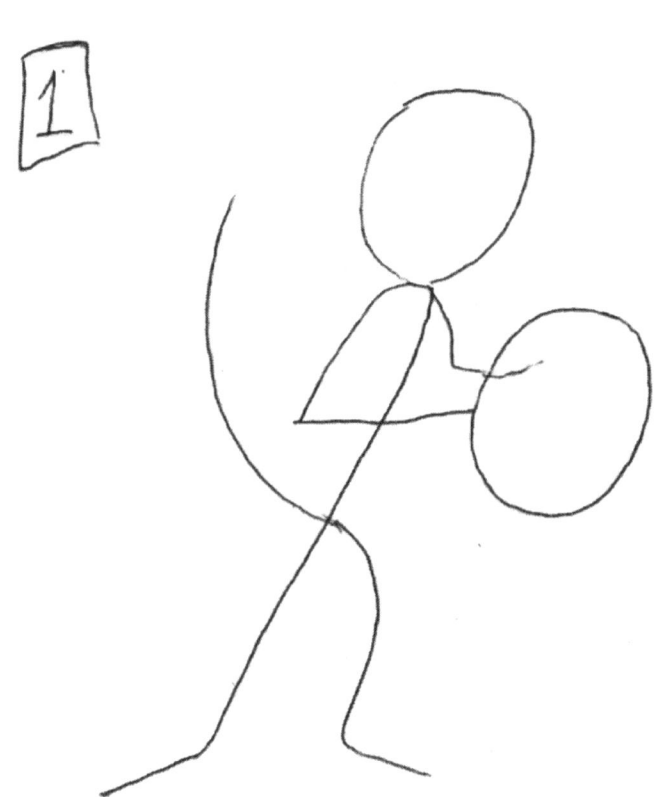

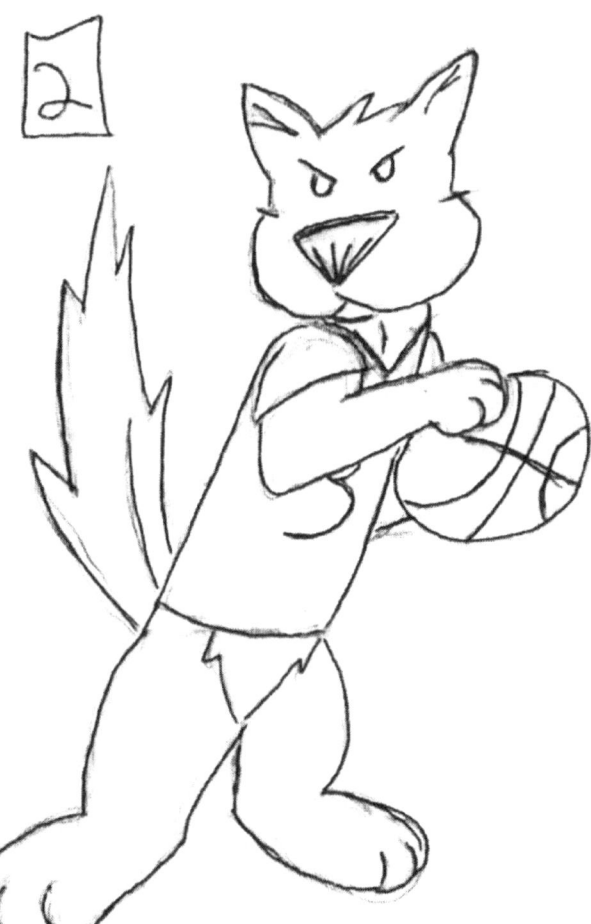

# Kung Fu Puppy

Often, when I have an idea of something I want to draw, but don't know exactly how to draw it, it is super helpful drawing a bunch of skeletons and then picking your favorite position. For example, I want draw a Kung Fu Puppy, but don't know exactly what position I want to draw him in, or what I want him to be doing, so I am going to experiment by drawing a bunch of skeletons.

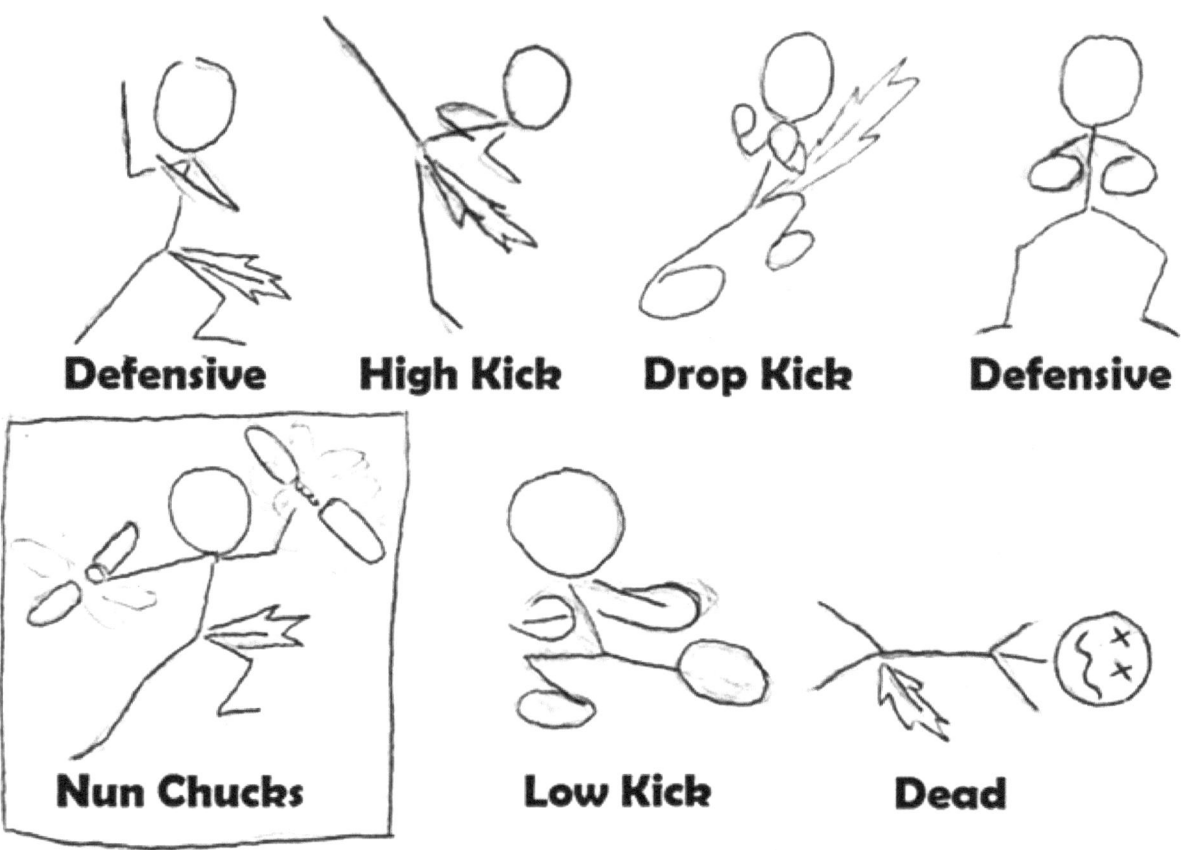

Defensive    High Kick    Drop Kick    Defensive

Nun Chucks    Low Kick    Dead

Drawing out the skeleton helps you visualize exactly what you want to draw. In this process you will probably make a bunch of changes and you might even find a whole new idea that you like even more. Can you imagine spending a long time working on a certain drawing and then in the end never being satisfied with it because you hate the position? This helps eliminate that problem.

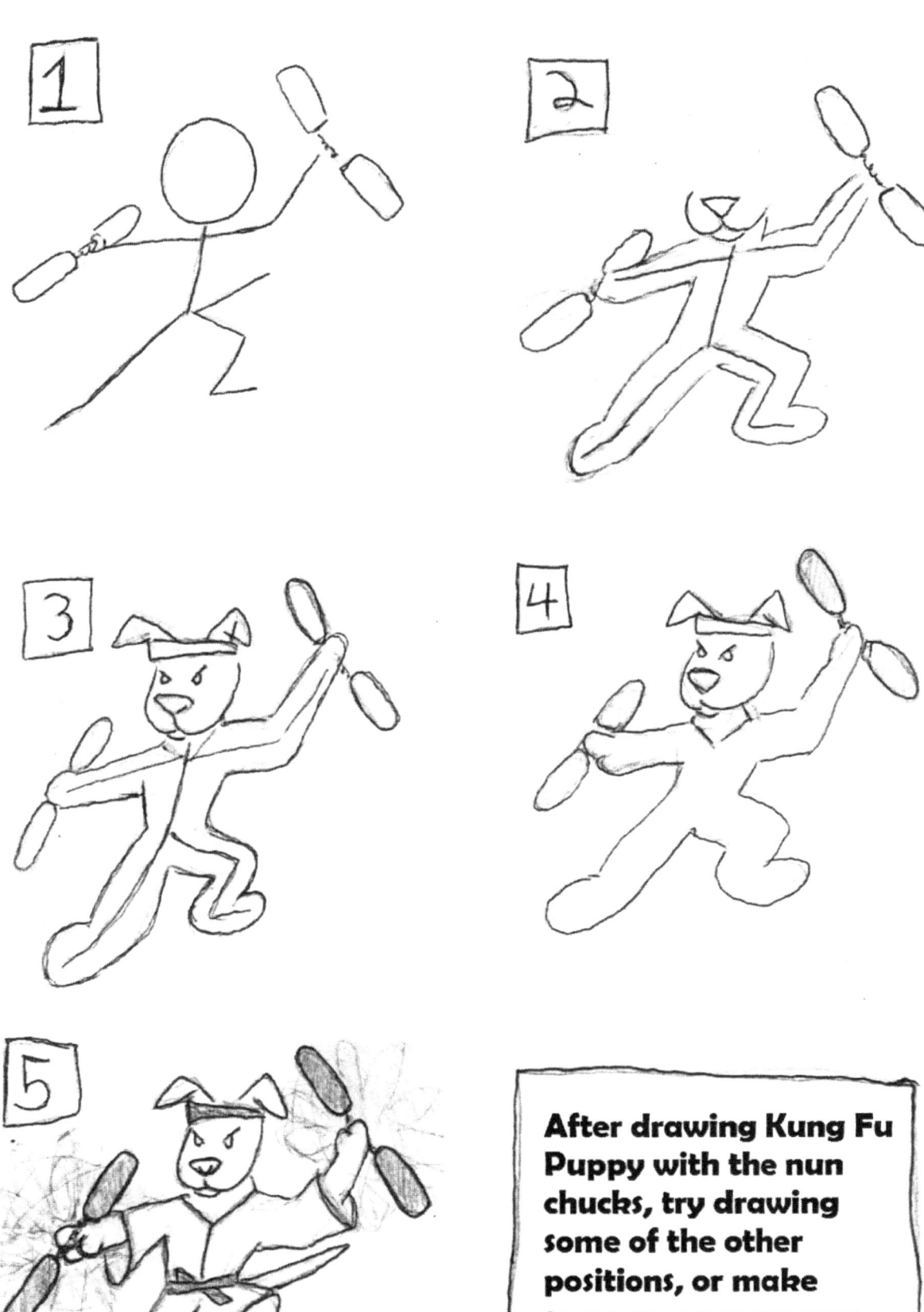

After drawing Kung Fu Puppy with the nun chucks, try drawing some of the other positions, or make some up on your own.

I don't always use skeletons, most of the time I draw a light bubble outline of what I want to draw, and then play Mr. Potato Head with my outline. Just remember, you are the artist and can draw in whatever way works best for you.

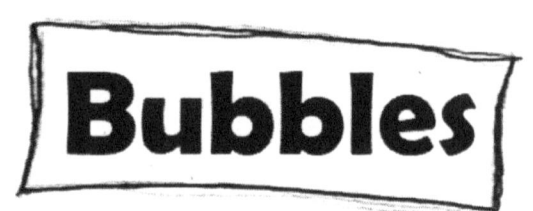

## Super Puppy

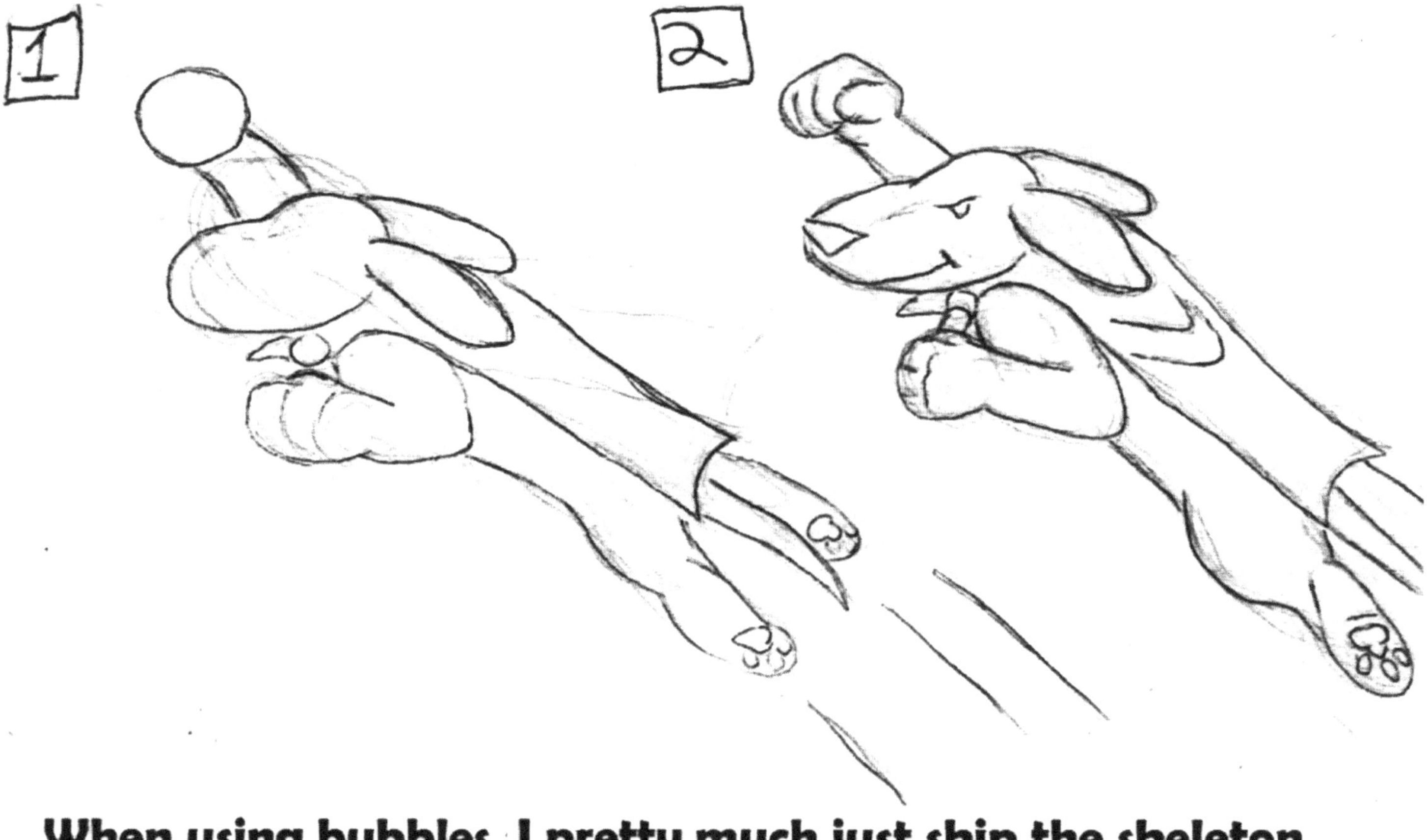

When using bubbles, I pretty much just skip the skeleton step and just start drawing an outline of the figure I want to draw. When you do this, draw it lightly first, sometimes it may take several tries to get it to where you want it, then darken the outline you like most and erase the old ones. This method can sometimes require more erasing, but like I said before, draw in whatever way works best for you.

**Another way to use bubbles is to look at a picture, like Chester here in this picture, draw an outline or shape of the dog and then fill it in with the details.**

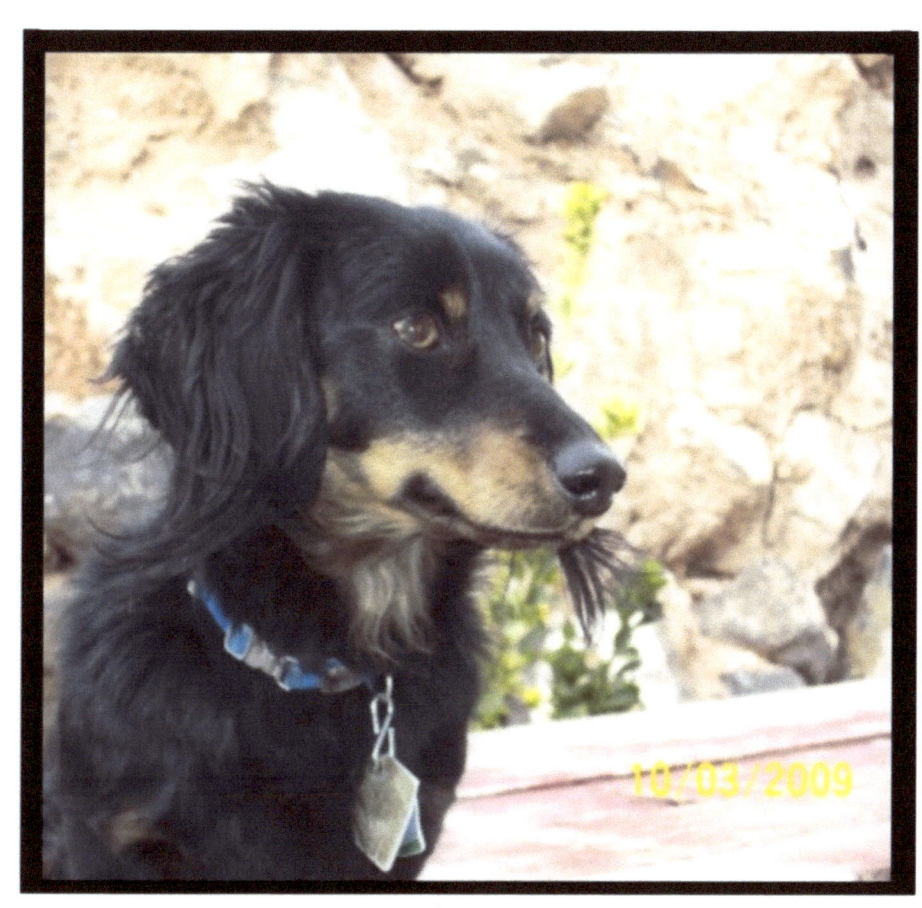

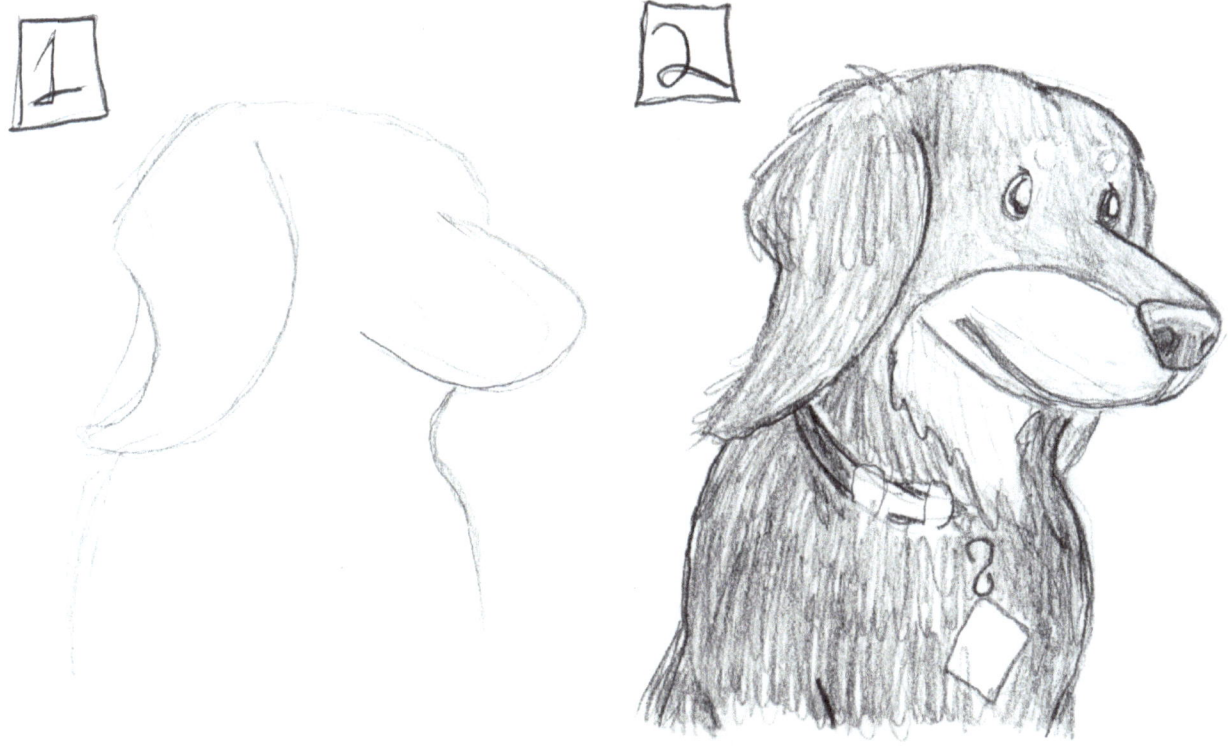

# Phase 3
# Individual Breeds

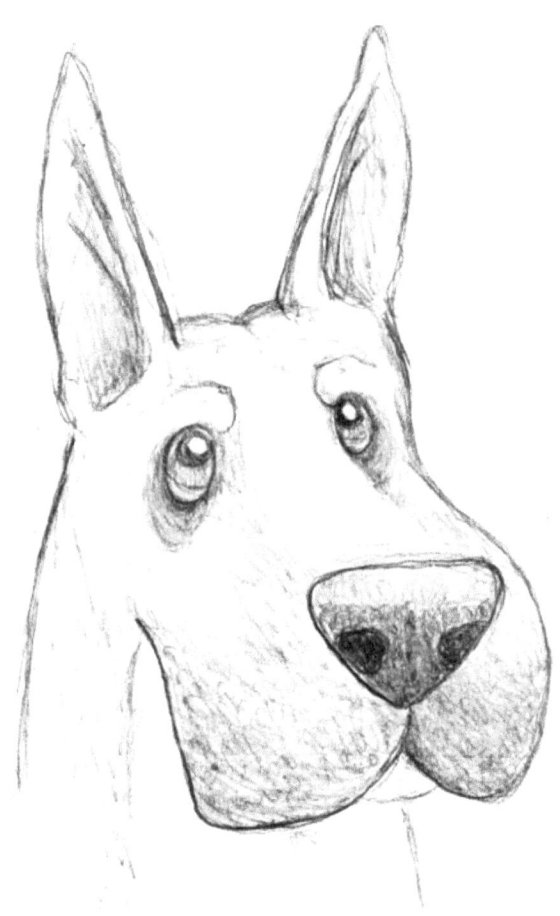

The overall goal of this book is to teach you to be able to draw dogs on your own without using any references. In Phase 3 you will notice that I no longer teach step by step how to draw each dog, that is because, congratulations, you no longer need it. In Phase 3 you take the skills you learned in Phases 1 and 2 and use them to draw the Phase 3 dogs.

# Great Danes

In Phase 3 we are modifying what we already know about how to draw a dog. As you already know, each breed has special characteristics that make that breed unique compared to every other dog. Phase 3 is all about memorizing those characteristics, so you will never need another reference again.

## Things to Remember:

- Tall pointy ears
- Long neck
- Really high elbows
- Really low knees
- Dark area around nose goes right back behind the eyes like a muzzle

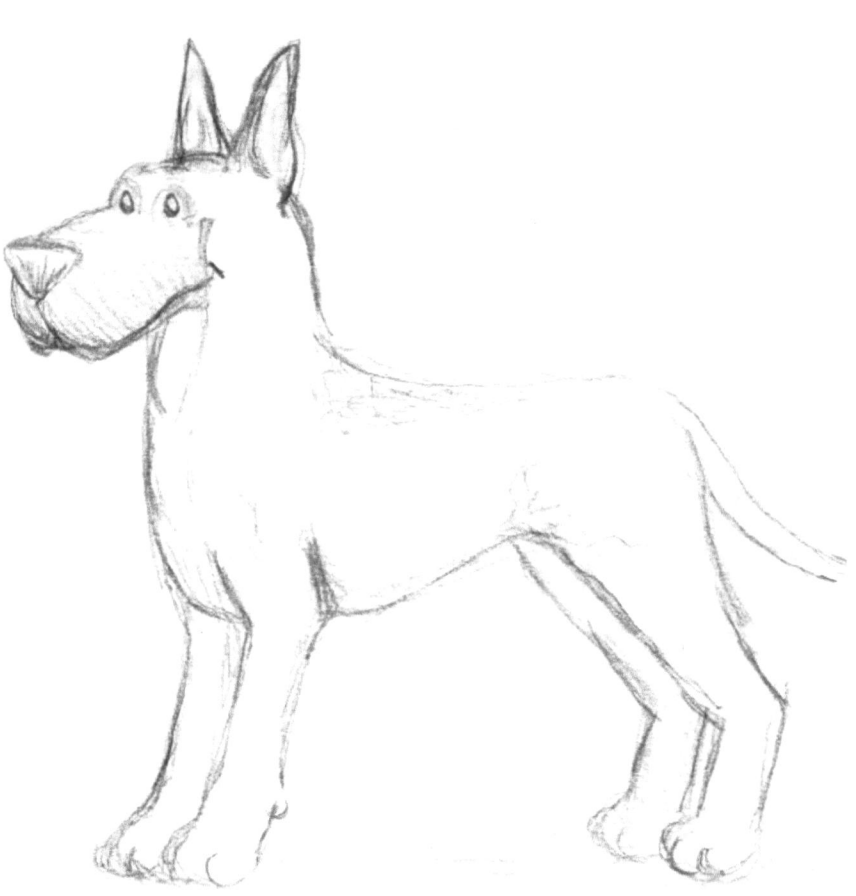

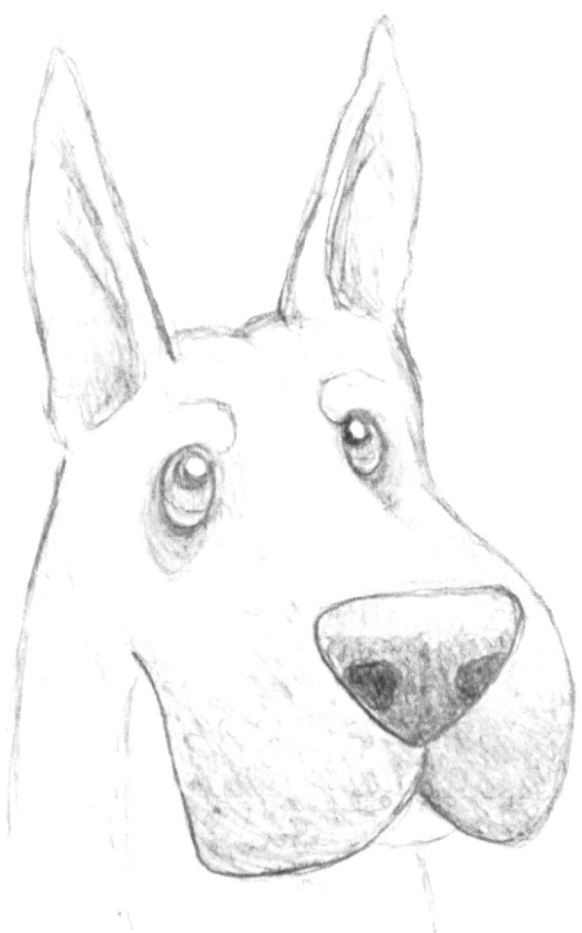

As you draw each dog, say each of the things to remember either out loud or in your mind as you draw each of those point.

# German Shepherd

**Things to Remember:**

-Dark Snout
-Pointy ears
-Long bushy tail

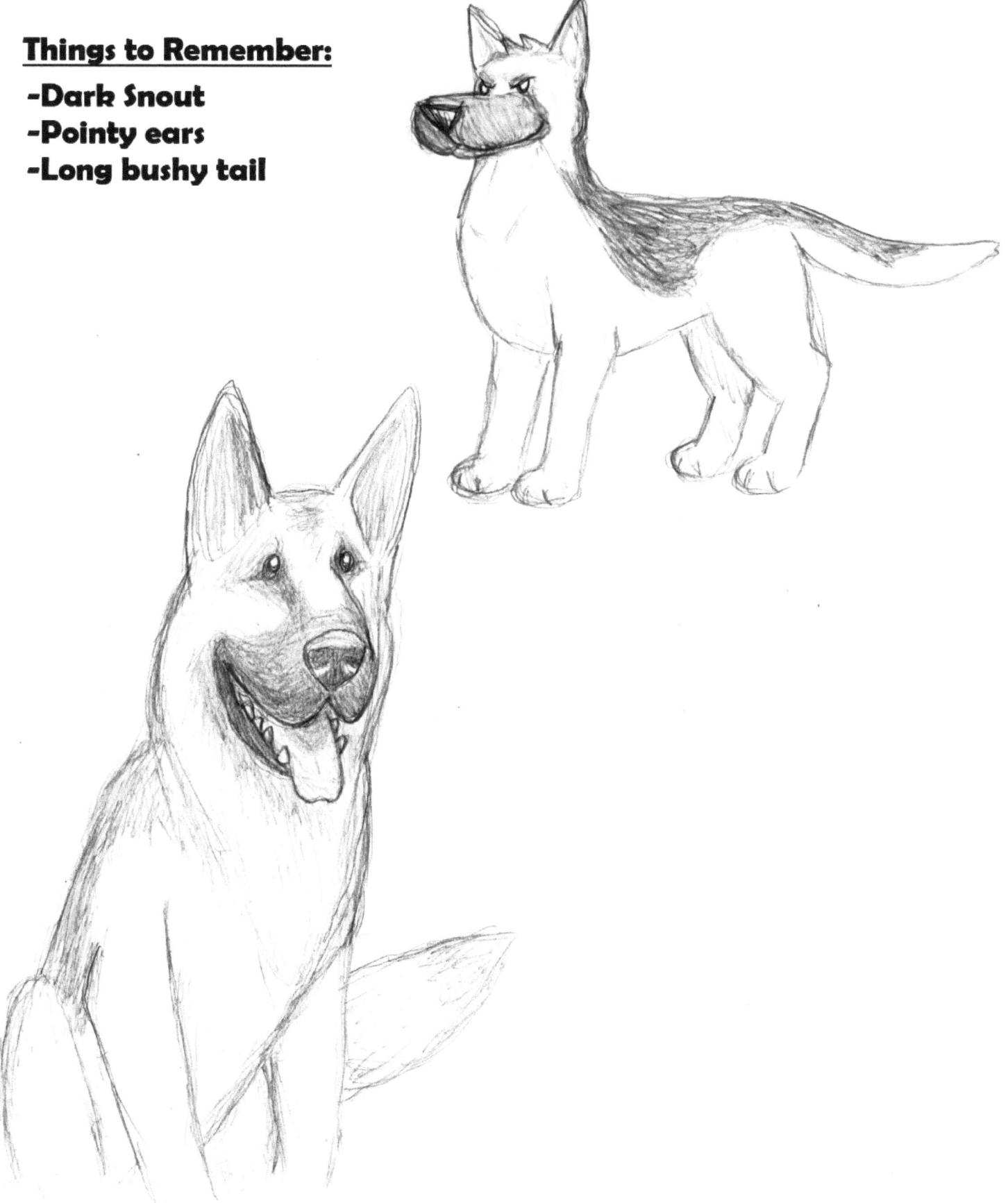

# English Bulldogs

## Things to Remember:

- More rounded nose
- Really short snout
- Eyes wide apart
- Short floppy ears
- Almost no neck
- Wide Shoulders
- Short Pudgy legs
- Back legs appear
  to be longer than
  the front legs
- Relatively straight
  hind legs
- The Hitler stach
  (The dark area
  under its nose)

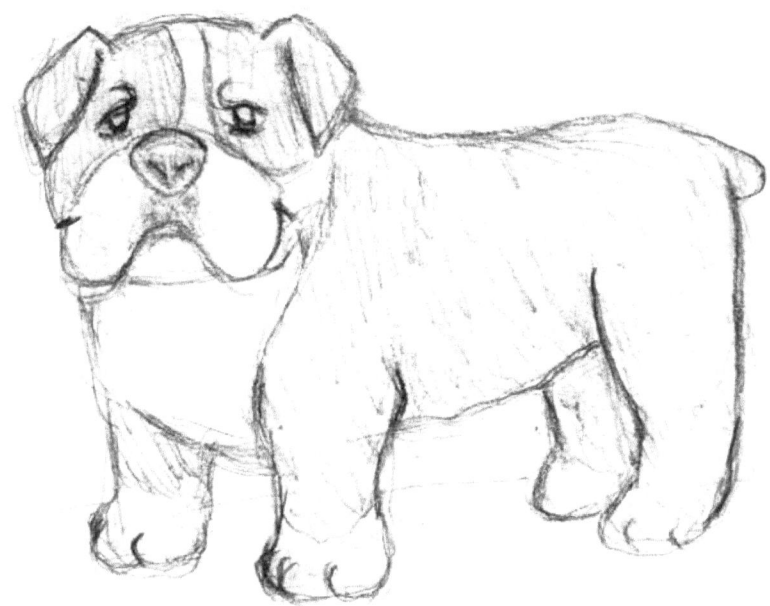

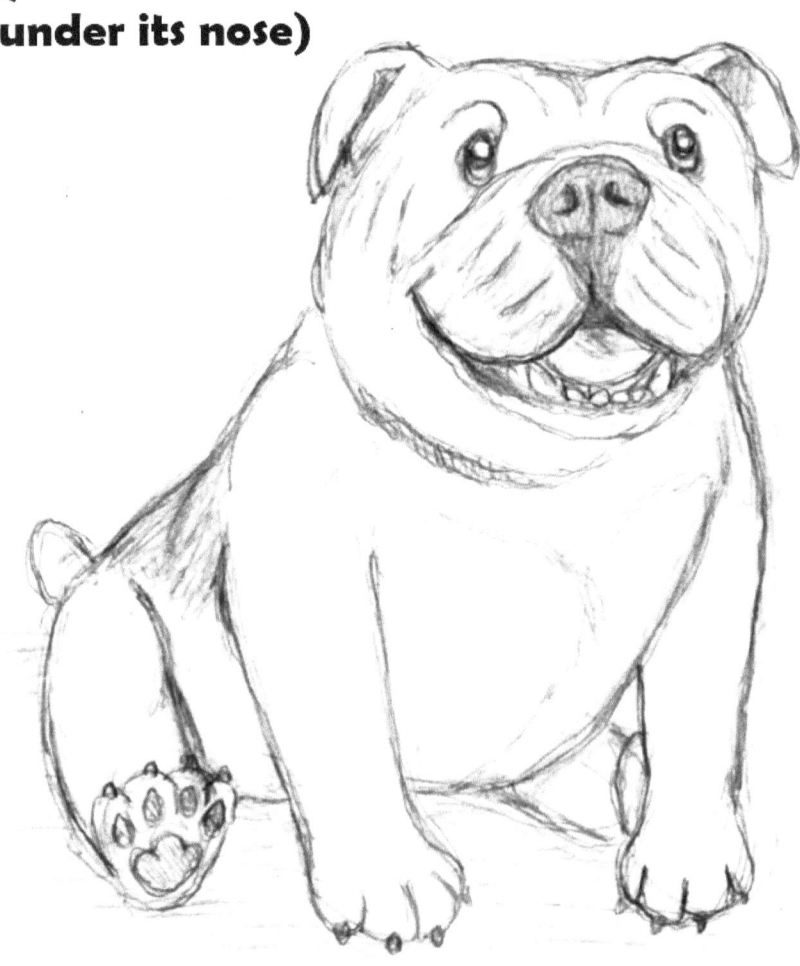

# Wrinkled Shar Pei

-Try drawing the dog
as an outline first, without
the wrinkles, then add them
in after.

- Super similar to a bulldog
-Short floppy ears
-Curly tail
-Eyes far apart
-Small forehead
-Short Snout
-Big pudgy paws

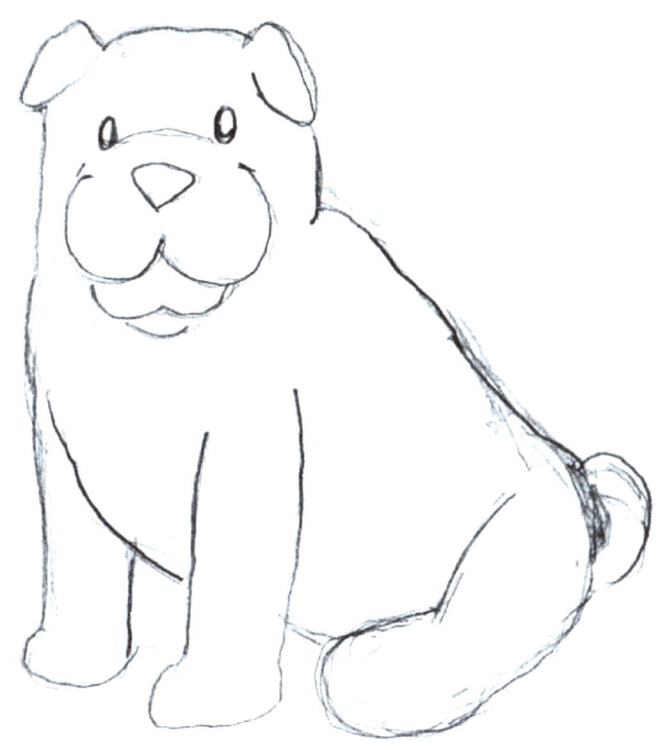

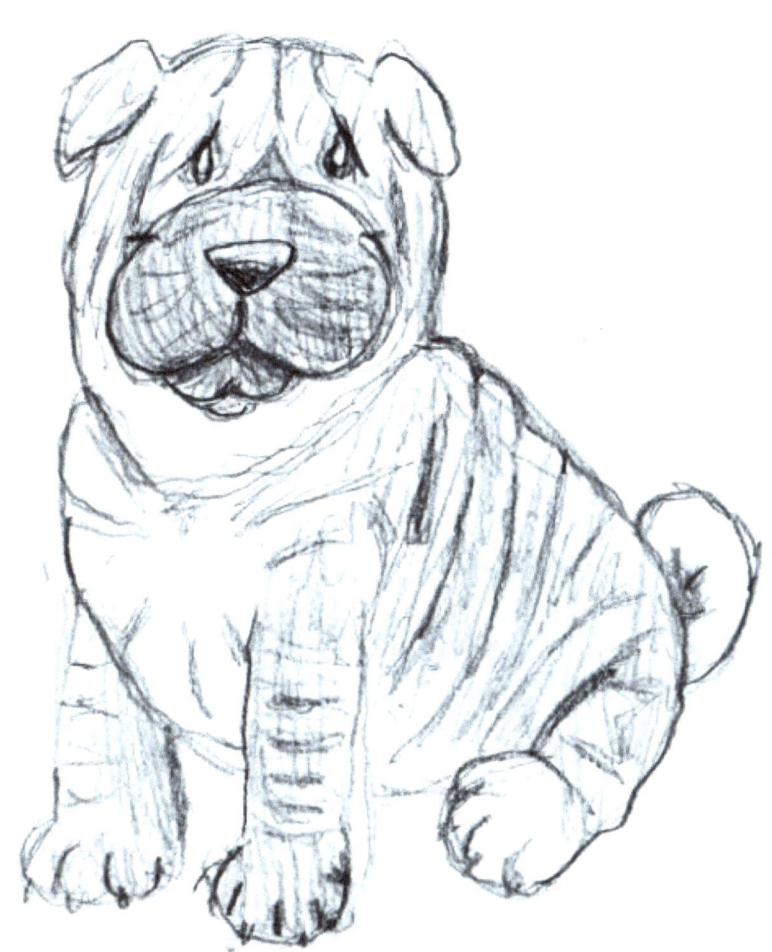

# Poodle

- Poodles generally have a pointy nose, although it depends on how furry their snout is.
- Big fluffy ears
- Long skinny legs
- Relatively straight hind legs

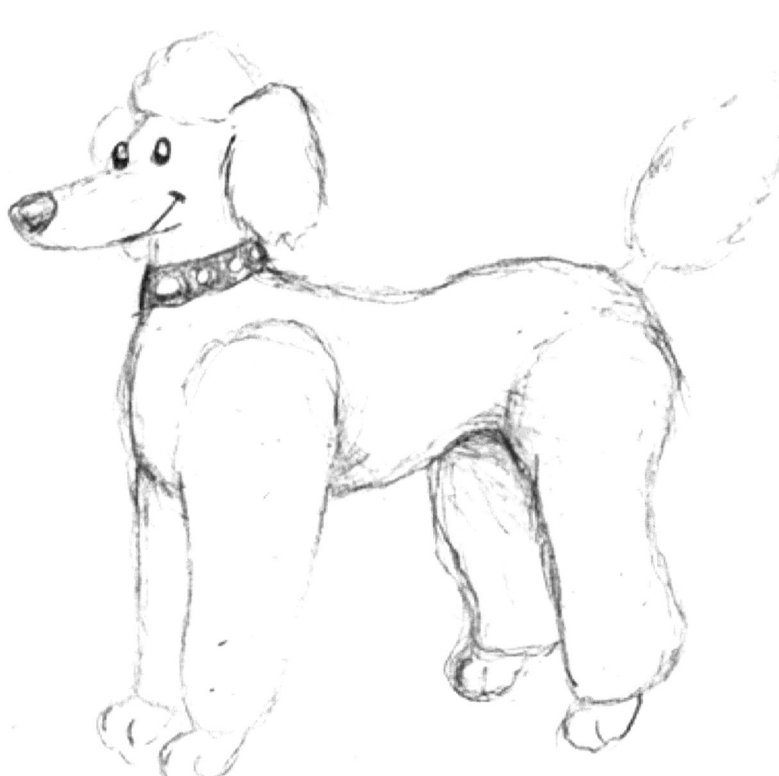

# Fancy Poodle

-Think of a woman with a fur hat and long fur coat
-Also take note how all of the small dots and dashes give the Poodle's fur it's texture. The more texture you have the more realistic your picture will become.

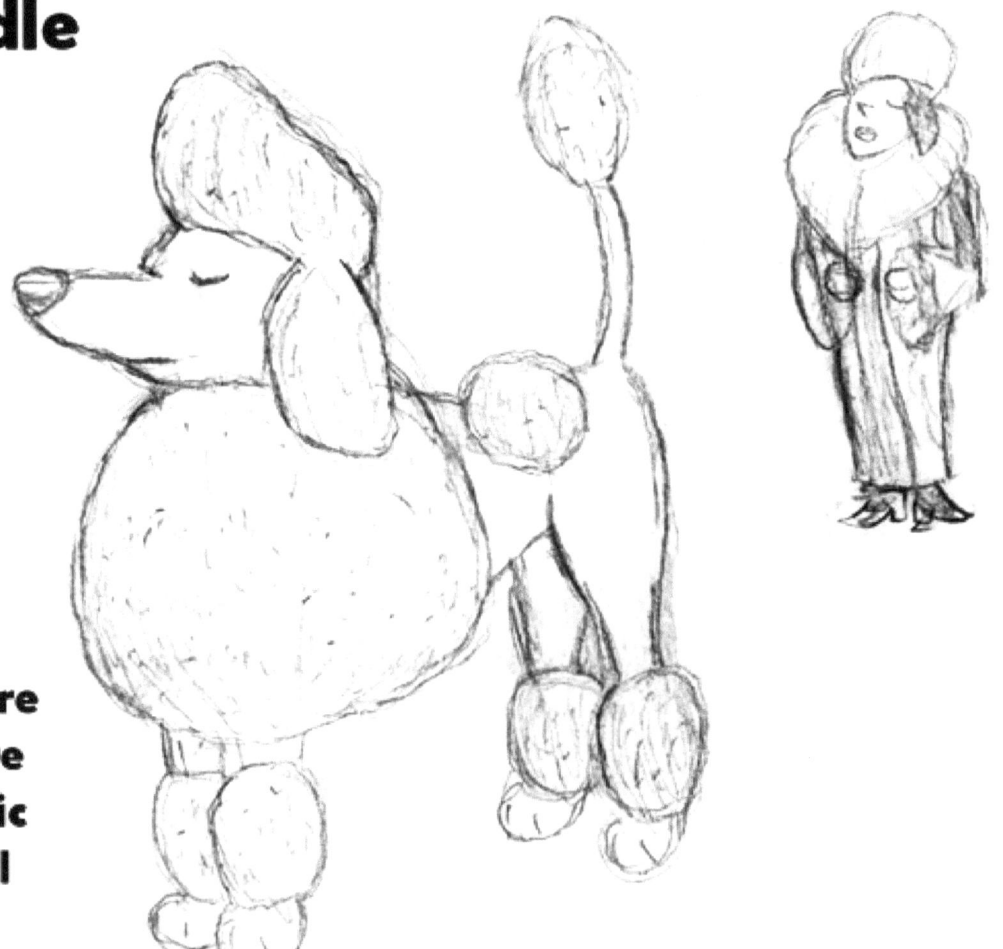

# Beagle

- Long floppy ears that hang down either to its jaw or past its jaw

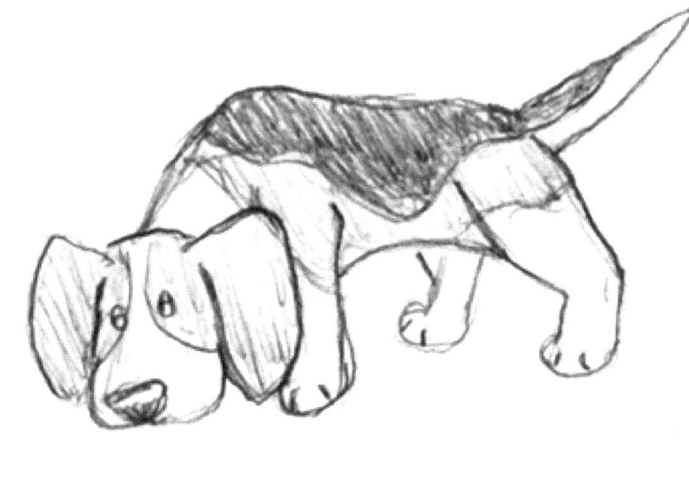

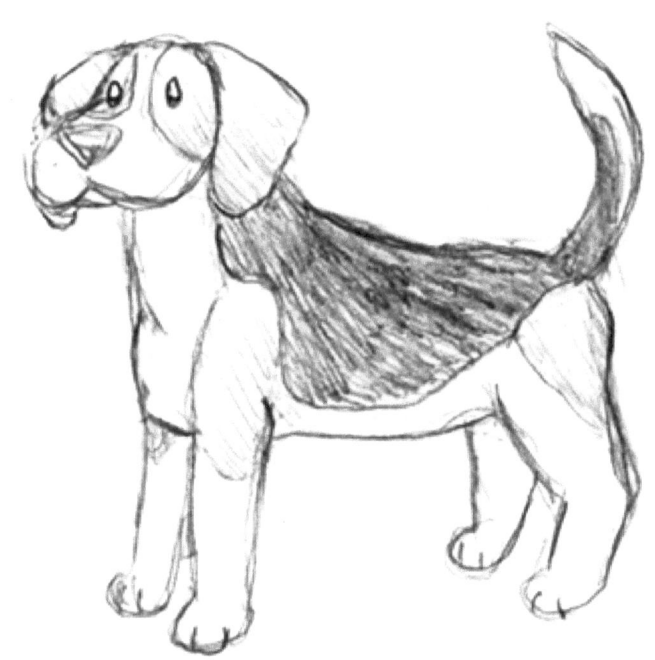

- An easy way to remember the markings of a Beagle is to think of a horse with a saddle and blinders.

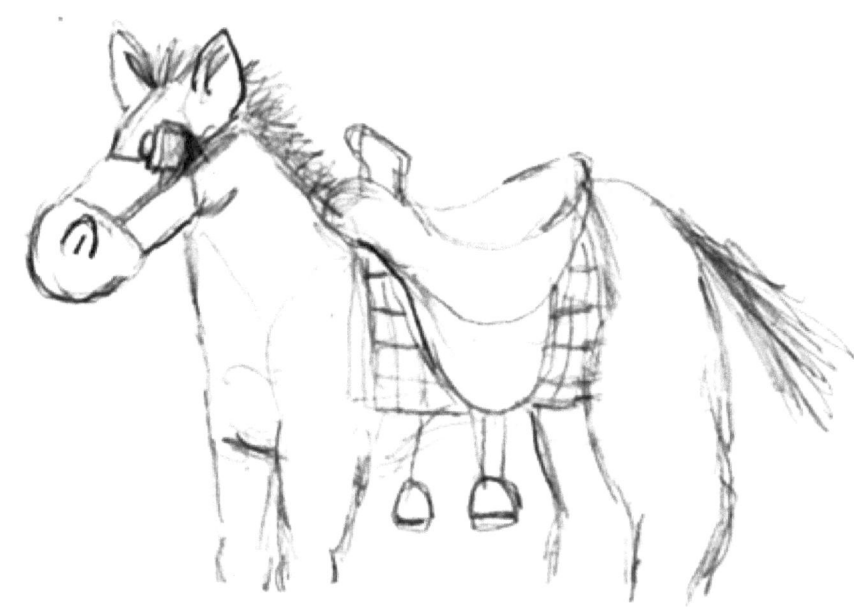

# Alaskan Husky

- Large Forehead
- Wide Neck
- Widows Peak
- Bushy curly
  tail

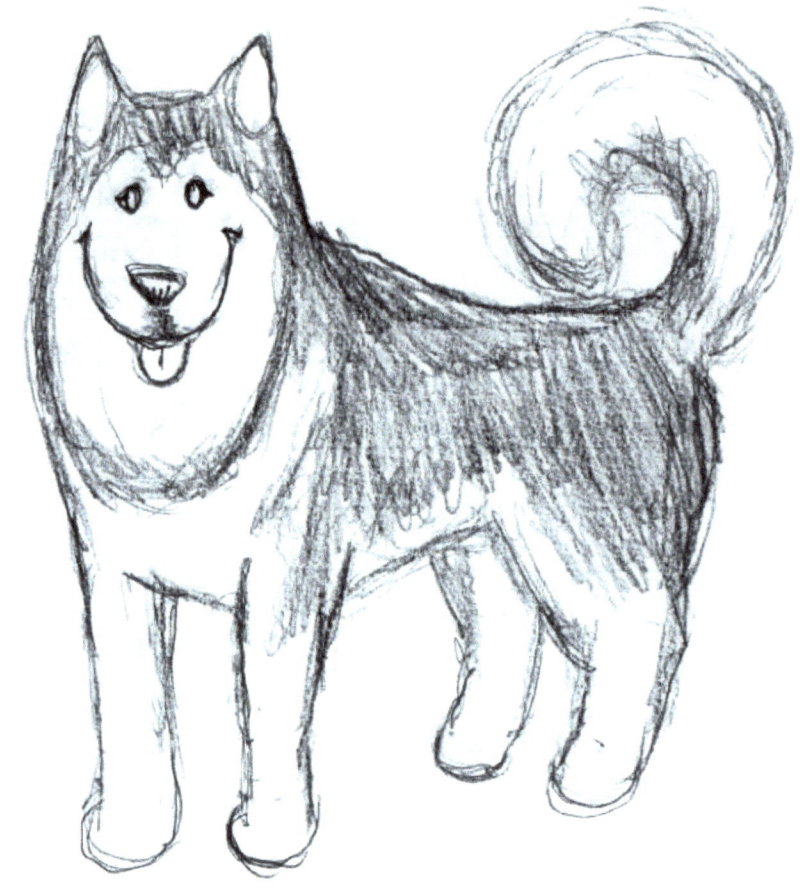

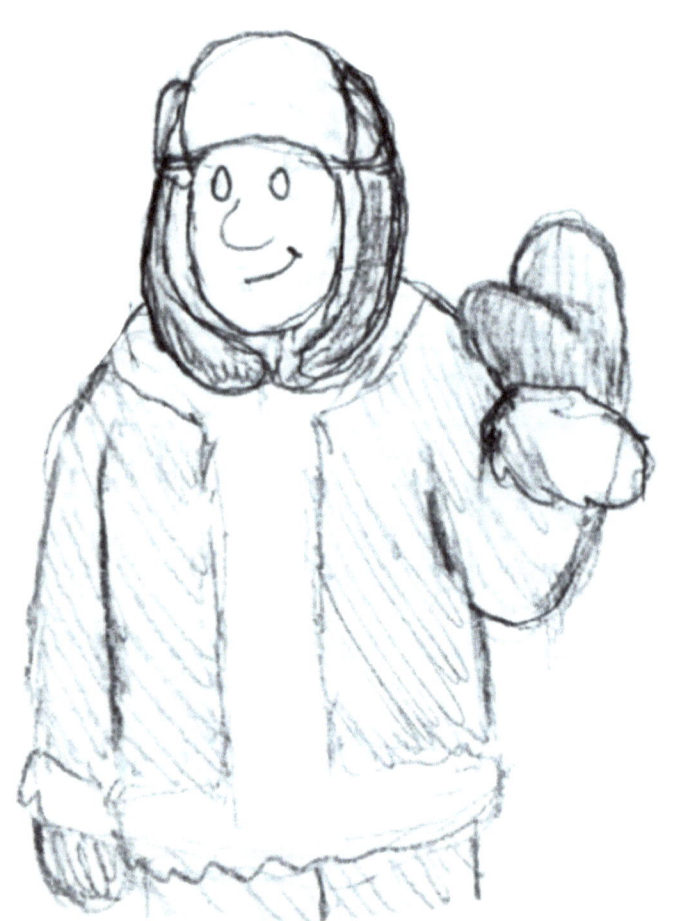

When drawing
the markings,
think of an
eskimo wearing
a hat.

# Grey Wolf

- Super Similar to the Husky, just different markings.

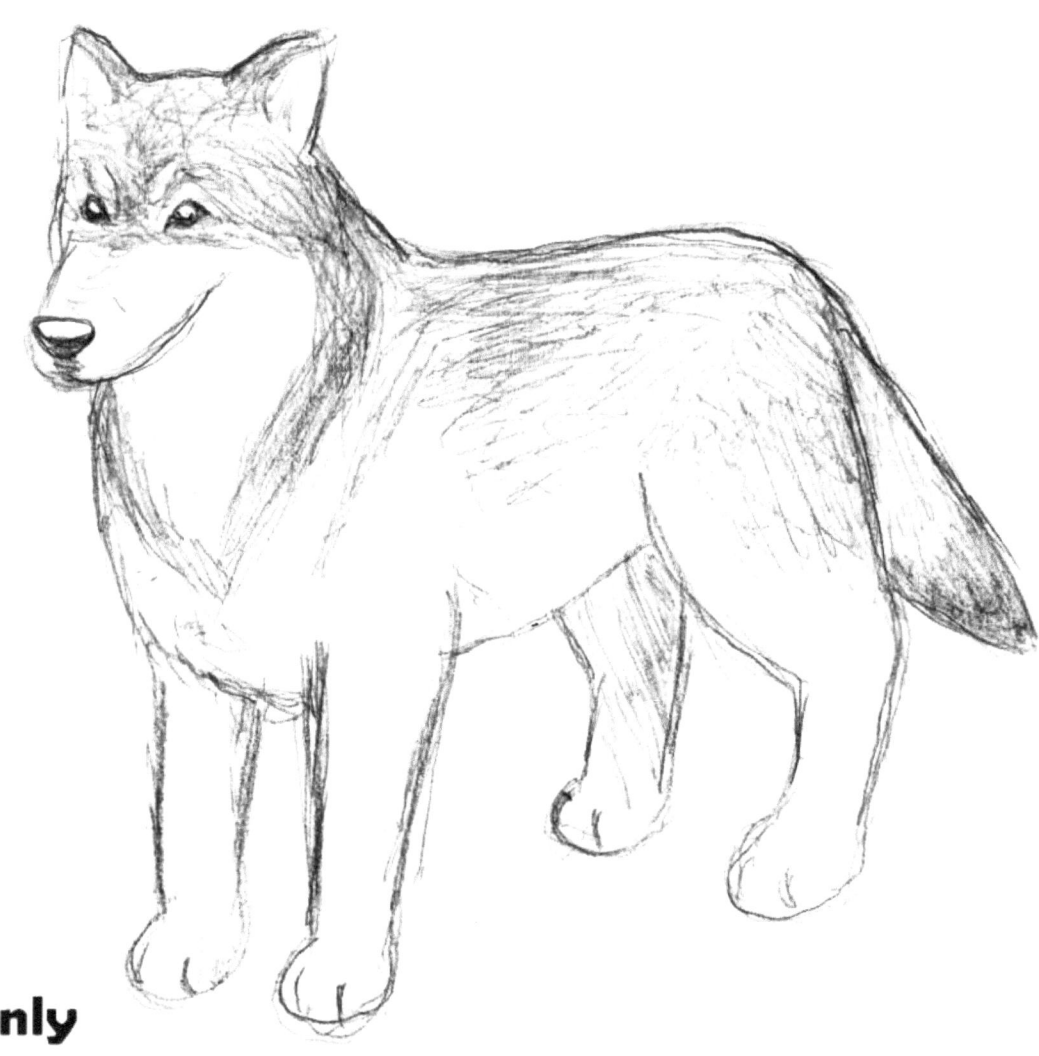

Wolves are commonly known as being bandits, so to help you remember their markings, think of a robber wearing a mask.

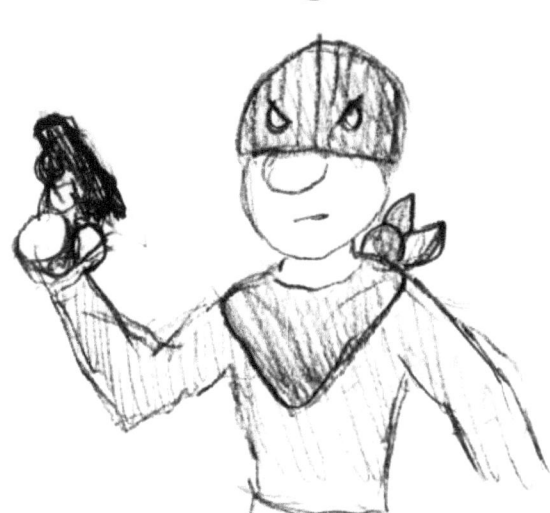

Either that or some kind of super hero.

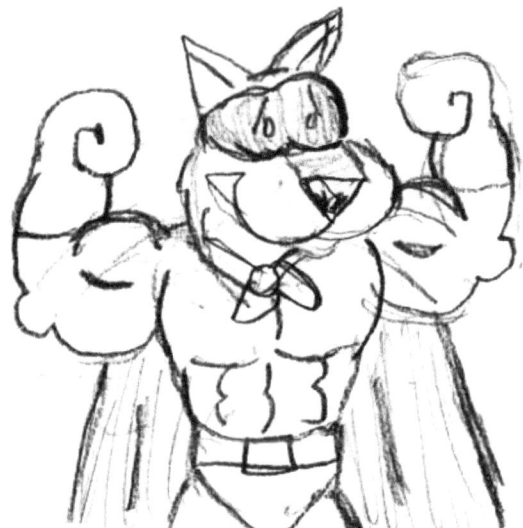

# Cocker Spaniel

- This is easier to draw without all of the fluffy fur first, and then add all of that on after.

- Also feel free to let the ears hang all the way down to the ground.

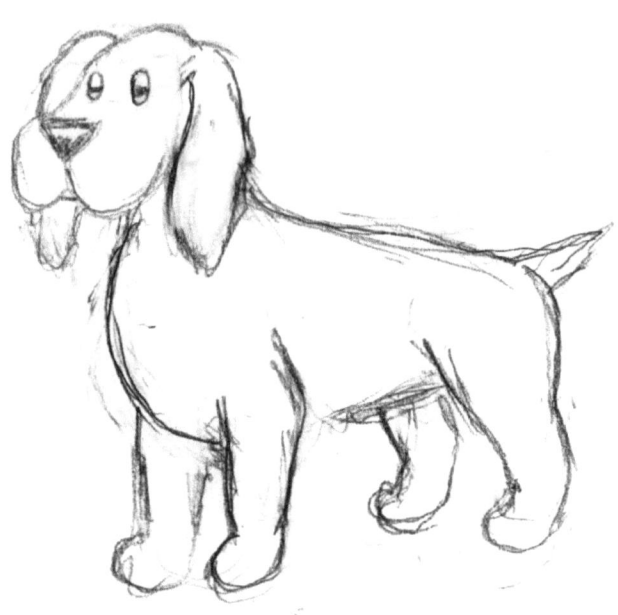

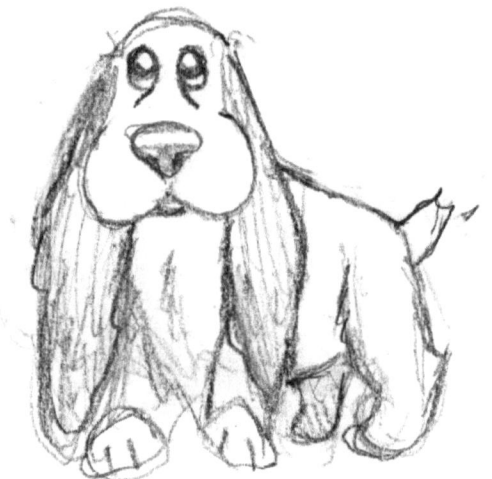

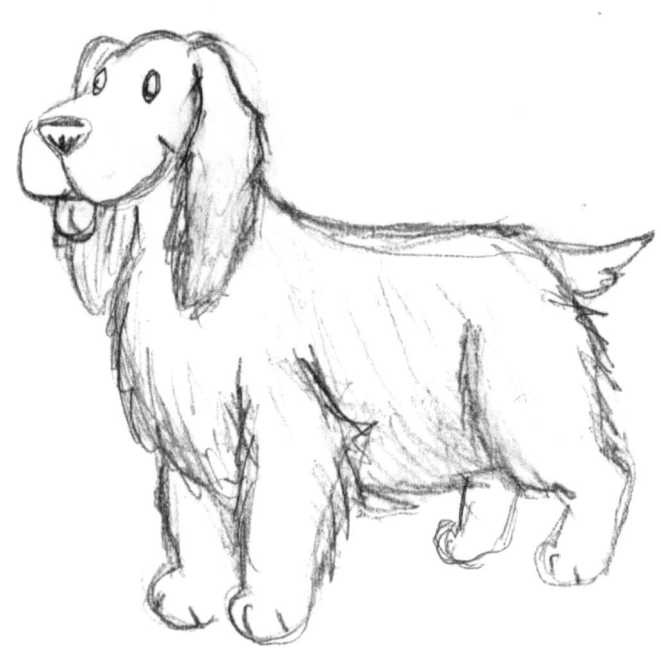

You are smart and I am sure you can figure out through your own observations what makes each dog unique and special.

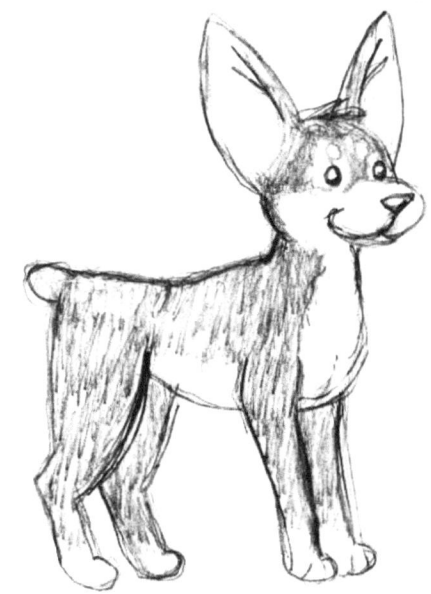

**Chihuahua**

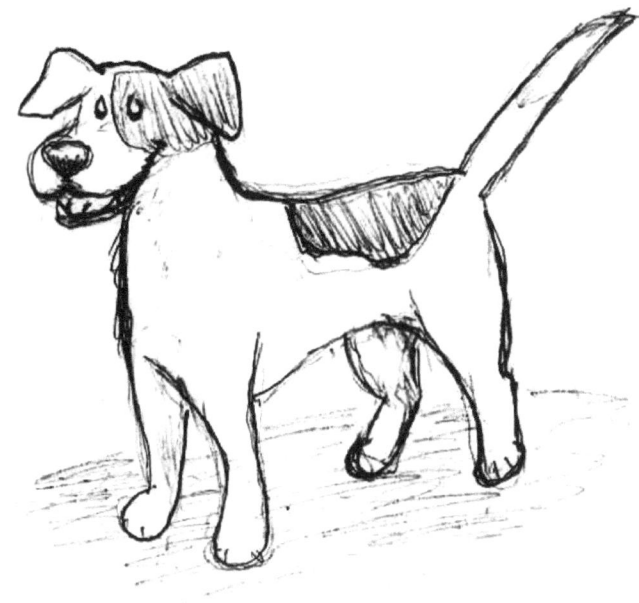

**Dalmatian**

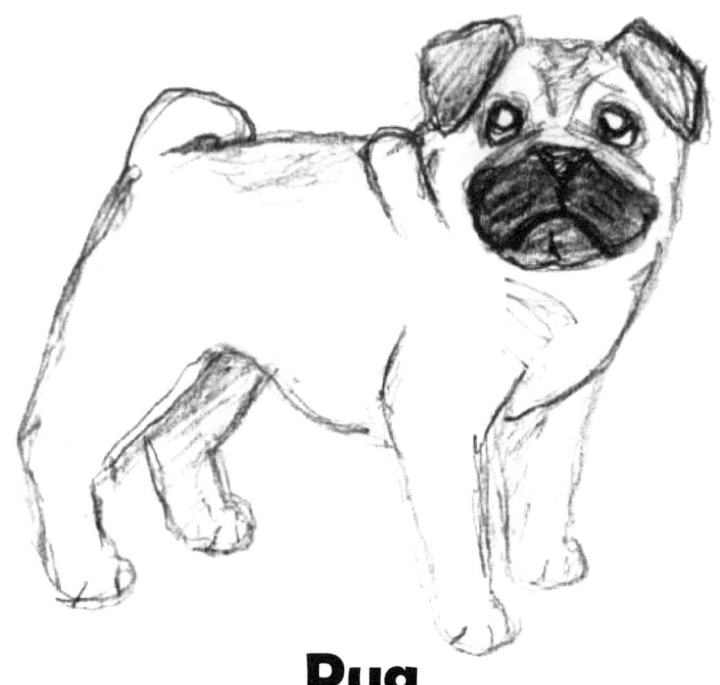

**Pug**

**Jack Russell Terrier**

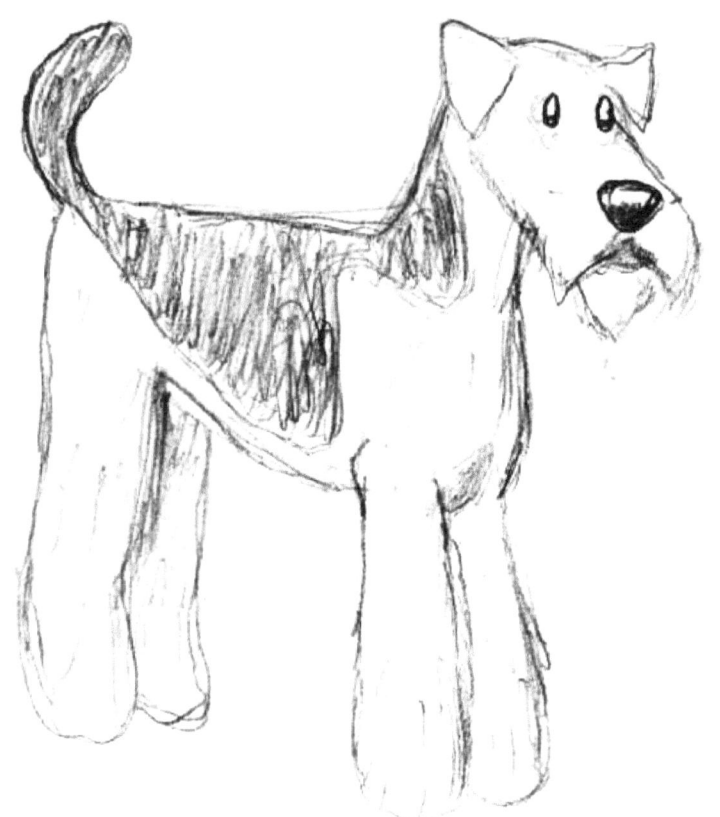

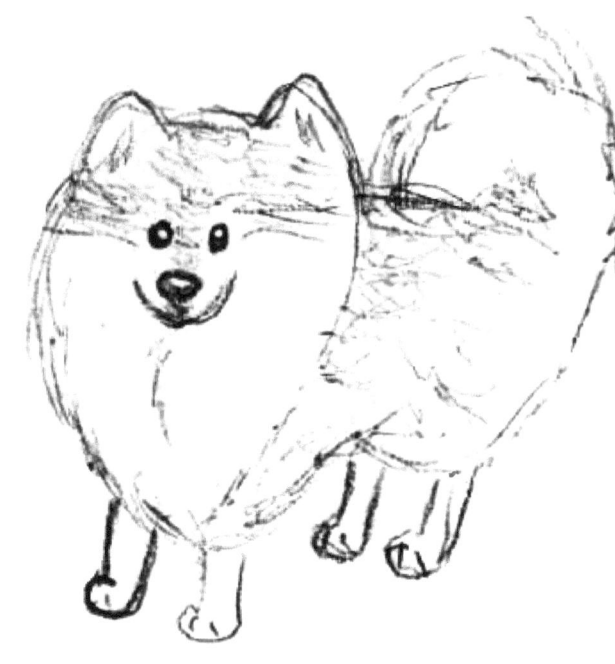

**Airedale Terrier**

**Pomeranian**

Though not a dog, look at how similar drawing a bear is to drawing a dog!

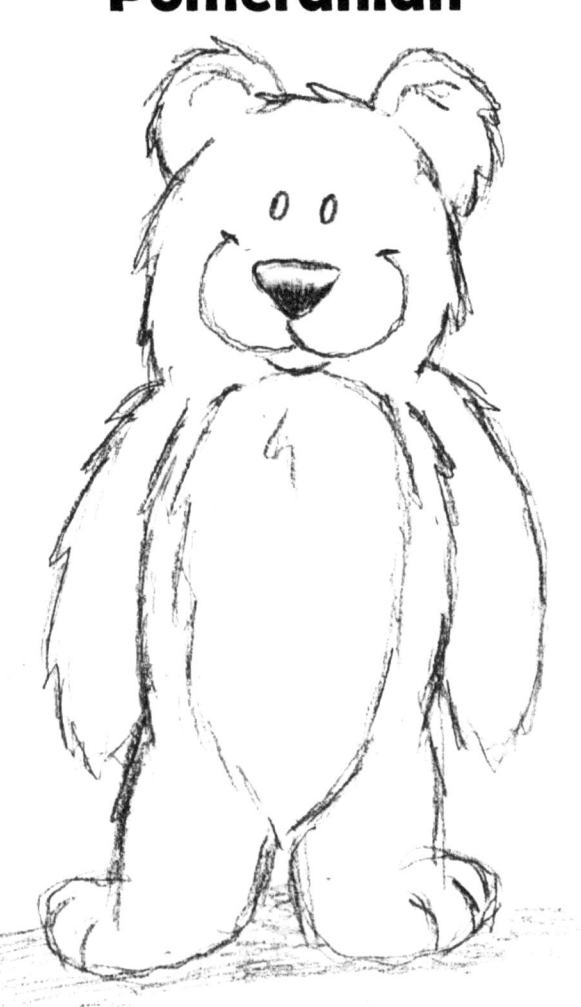

There are way too many types of dogs in order for me to have them all in this book.

From here on out, the next best way to continue your growth is to study from life.

It makes sense, if you want your drawings to look more lifelike, you have to learn how to draw by using real life models. If you want to learn how to draw a realistic looking dog, go find a real dog and draw it. Your local animal shelter continually has all sorts of different kinds of dogs both young and old.

_The key to learning how to draw them well without needing them to be continually at your side, or being entirely dependent on photos, is noticing and memorizing the simple shapes and memorizing the shortcuts._

# I took this picture at my local animal shelter

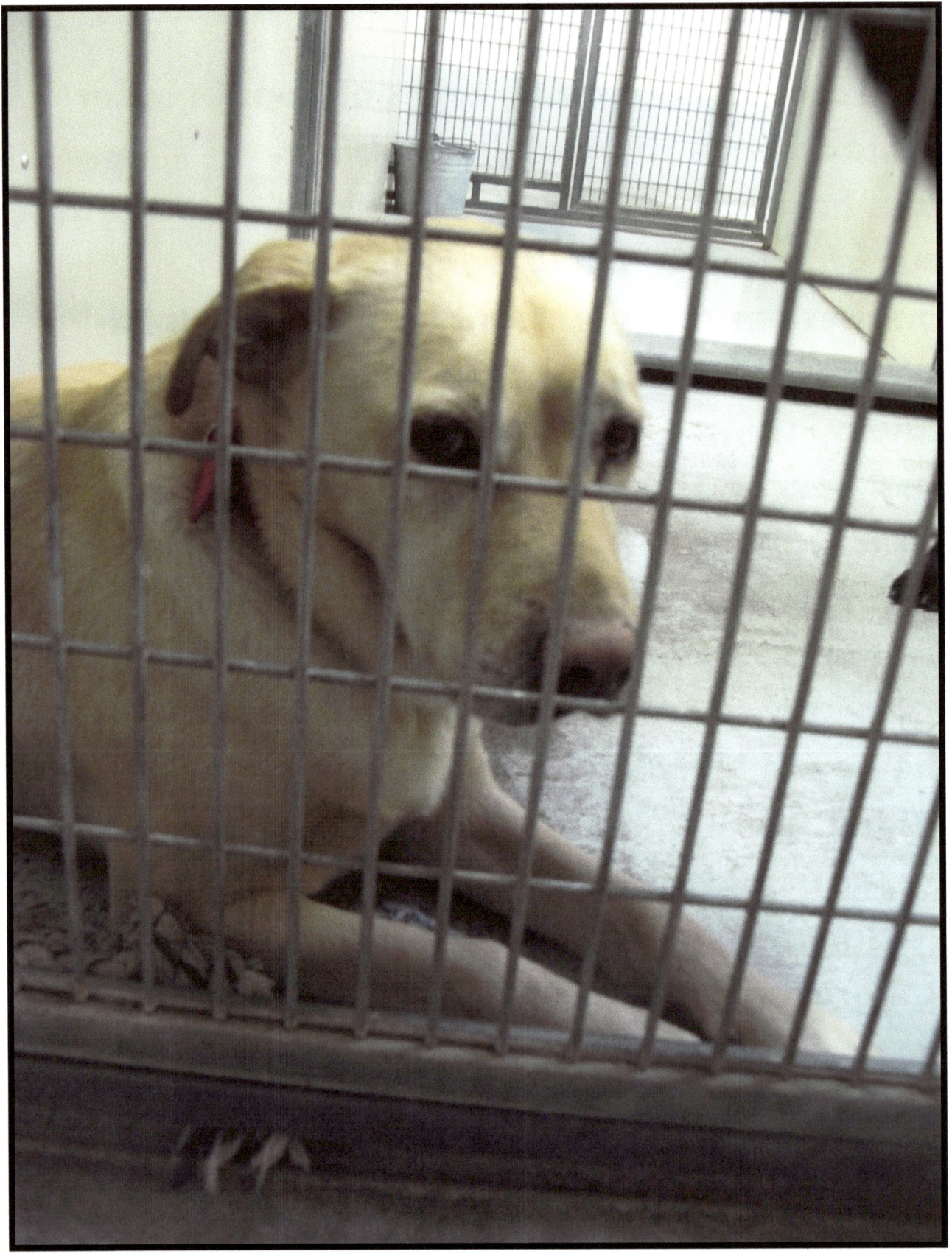

It may be a little heartbreaking to see so many animals in cages, but if you think about it, if you are drawing the animals at the animal shelter and showing your photos and drawings to your friends and family, you are raising awareness and that will make a difference and help save lives. Just remember a problem that is out of sight and out of mind does not get fixed and a dog that no one knows about does not get adopted.

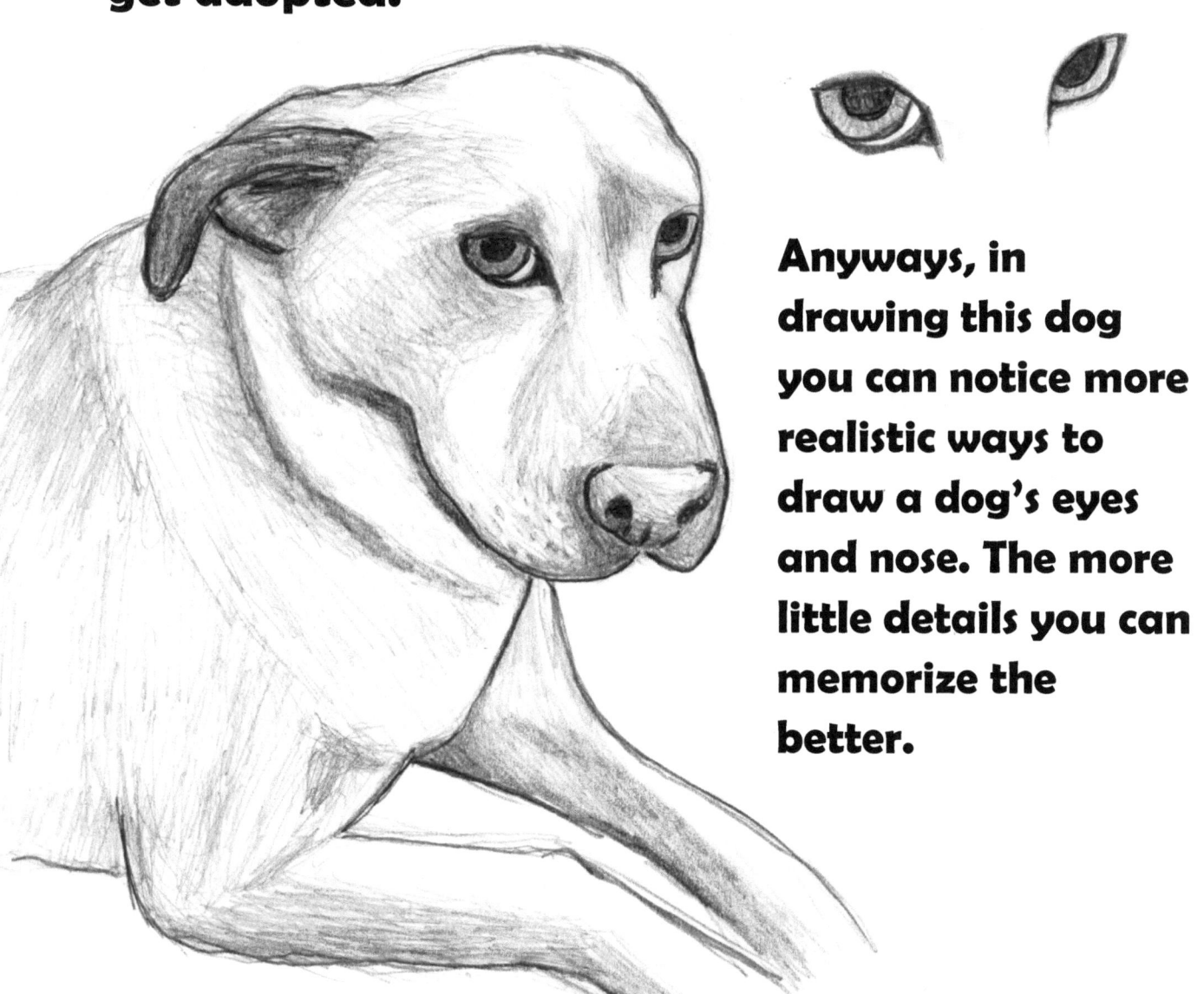

Anyways, in drawing this dog you can notice more realistic ways to draw a dog's eyes and nose. The more little details you can memorize the better.

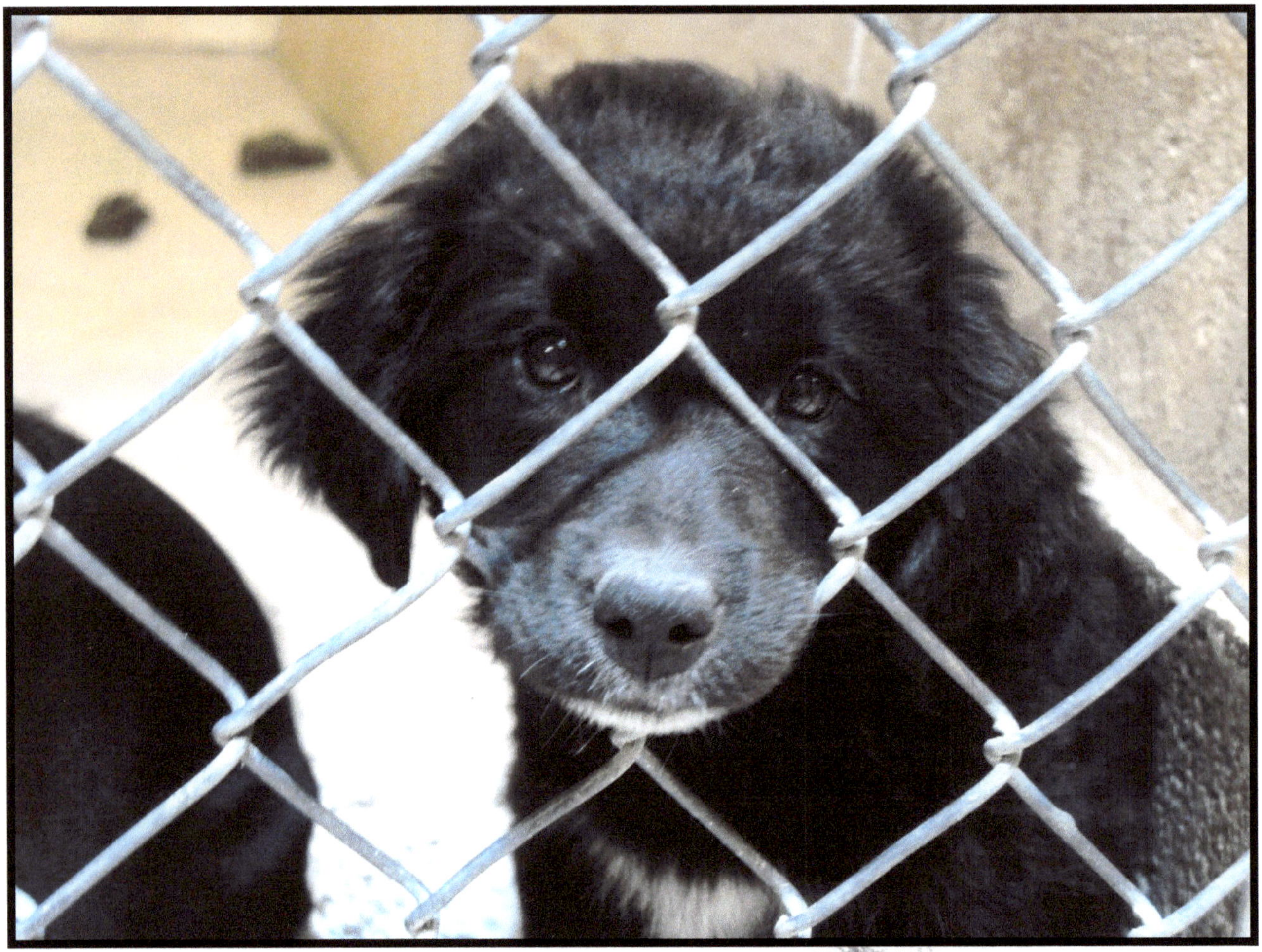

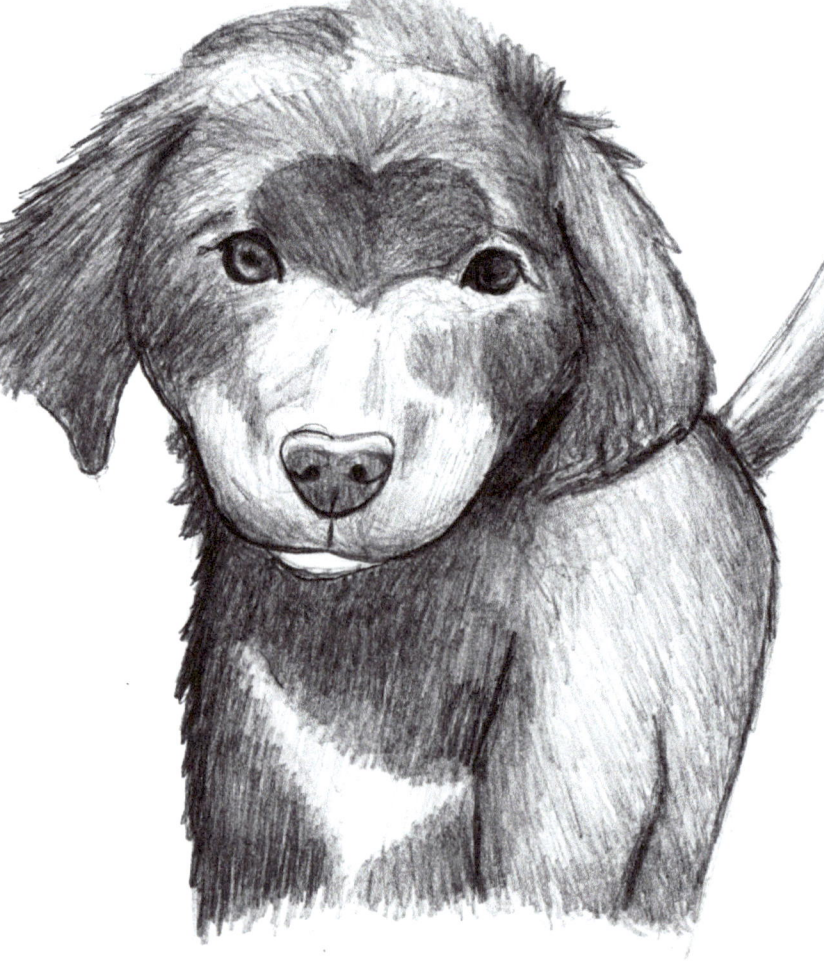

Remember,
just like it is with
people, not every
dog's eyes look
exactly the
same.

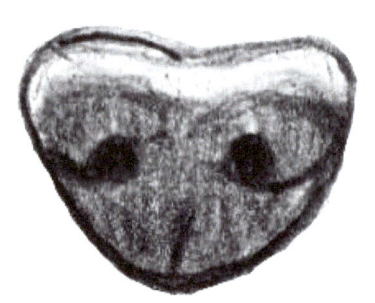

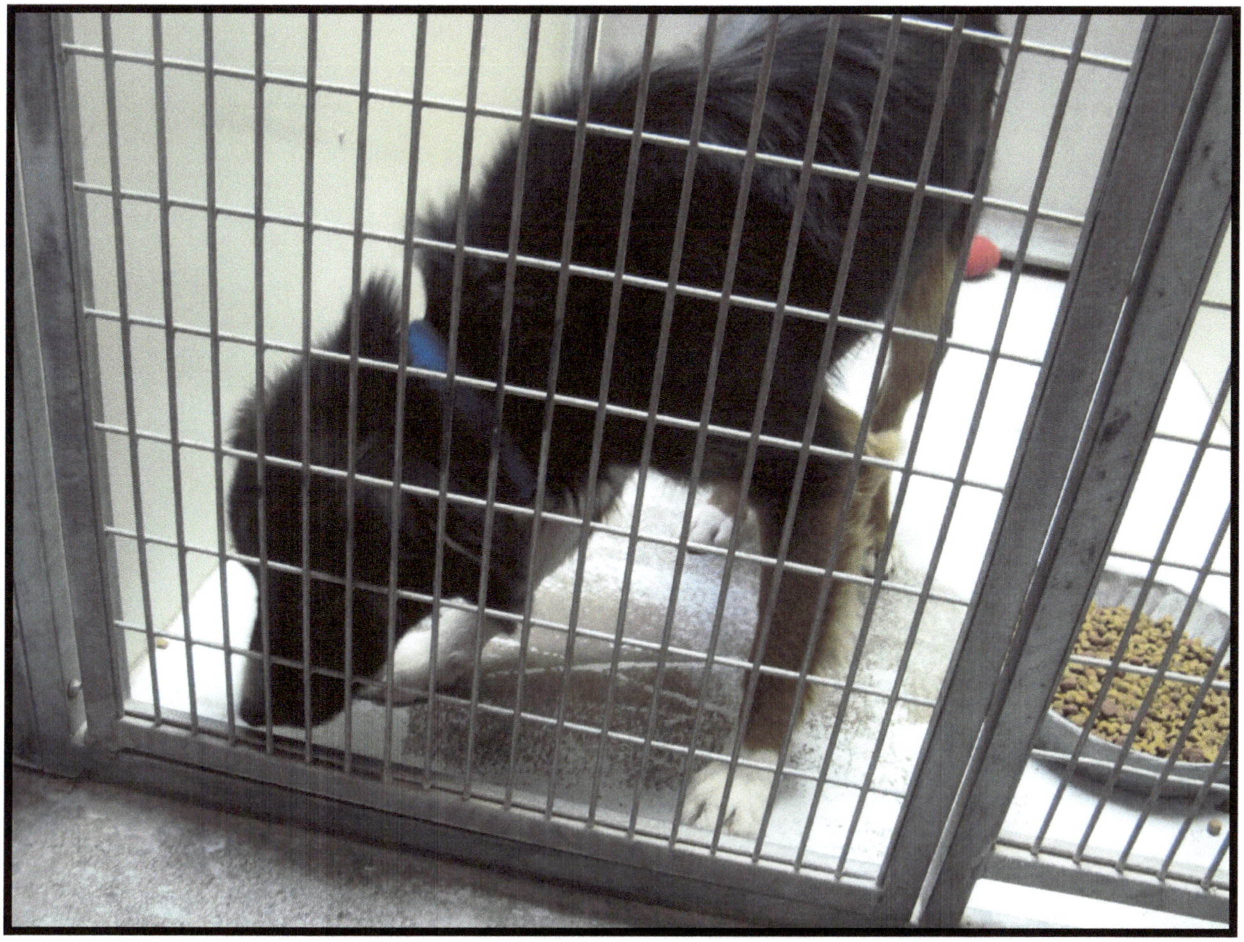

Drawing from life can also help you observe and explore different positions that can be difficult to visualize in your mind alone.

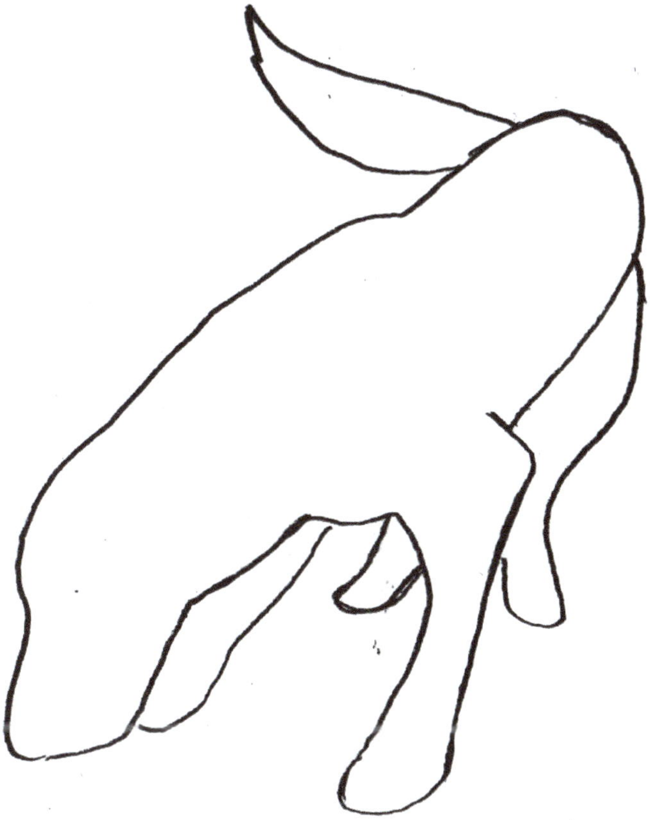

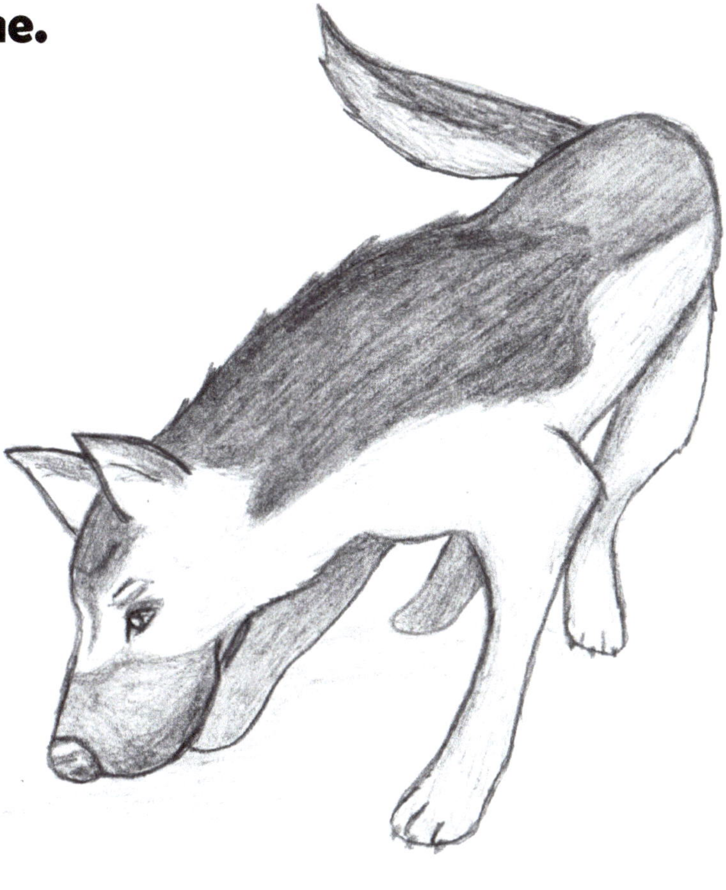

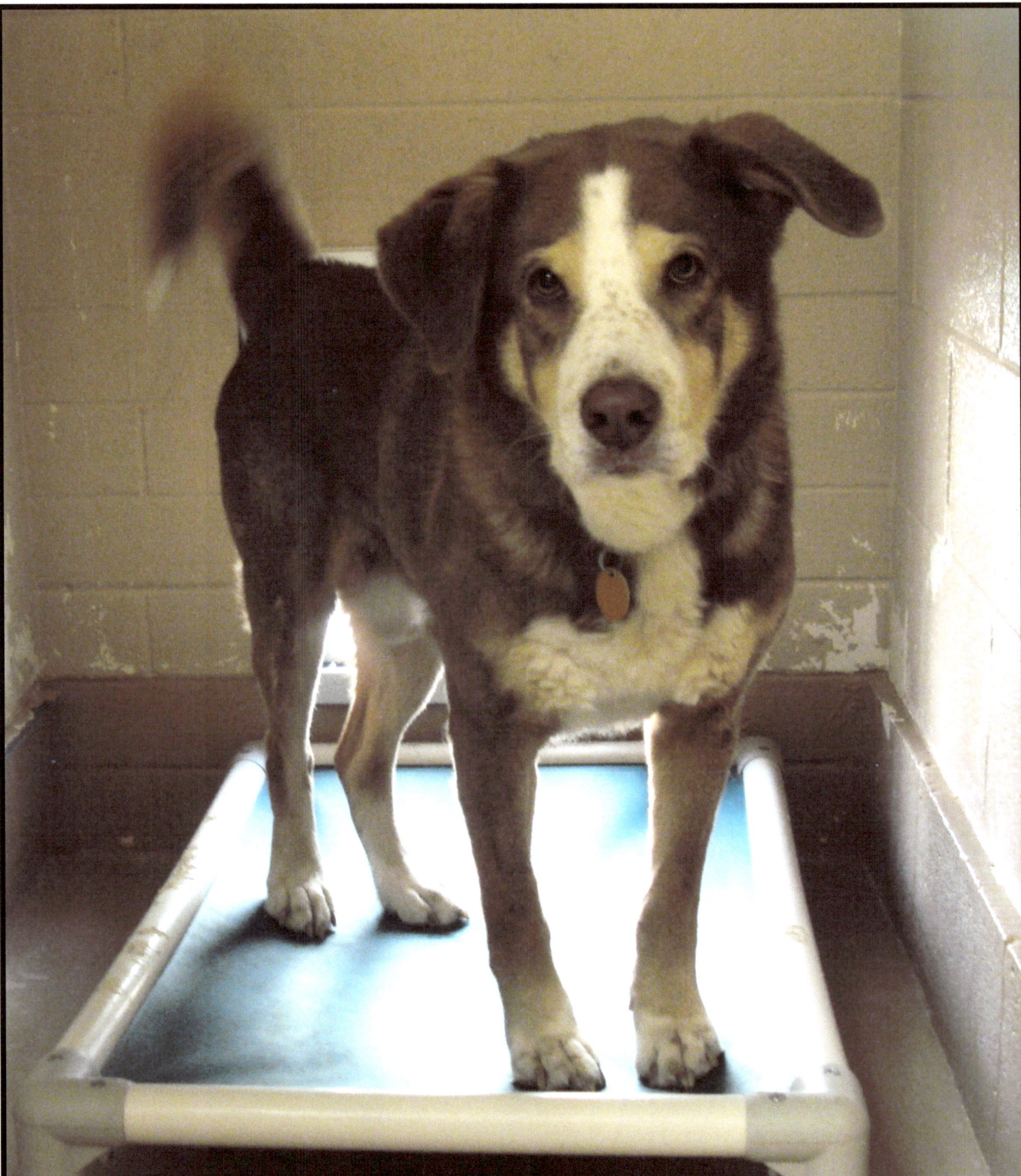

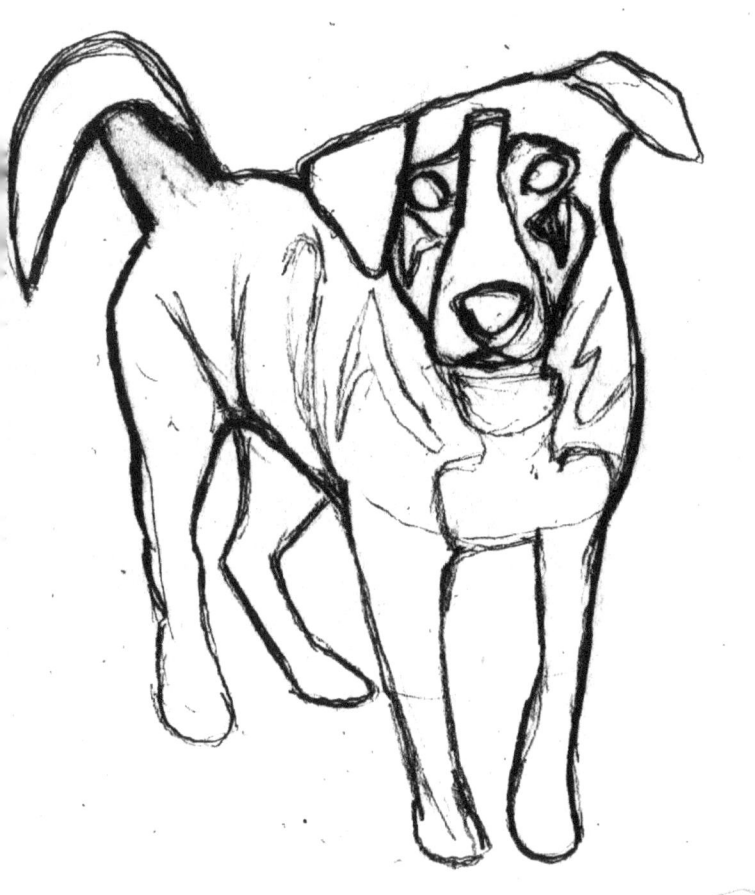

REMEMBER, REMEMBER, REMEMBER, it is all about looking for the simple shapes. Most mistakes that take place when drawing from life happen when the artist fails to recognize the simple shapes. With this being so, the basic outline of your drawing winds up being the most important part of your drawing.

It may take you some time to master this, but YOU <u>CAN</u> DO IT!

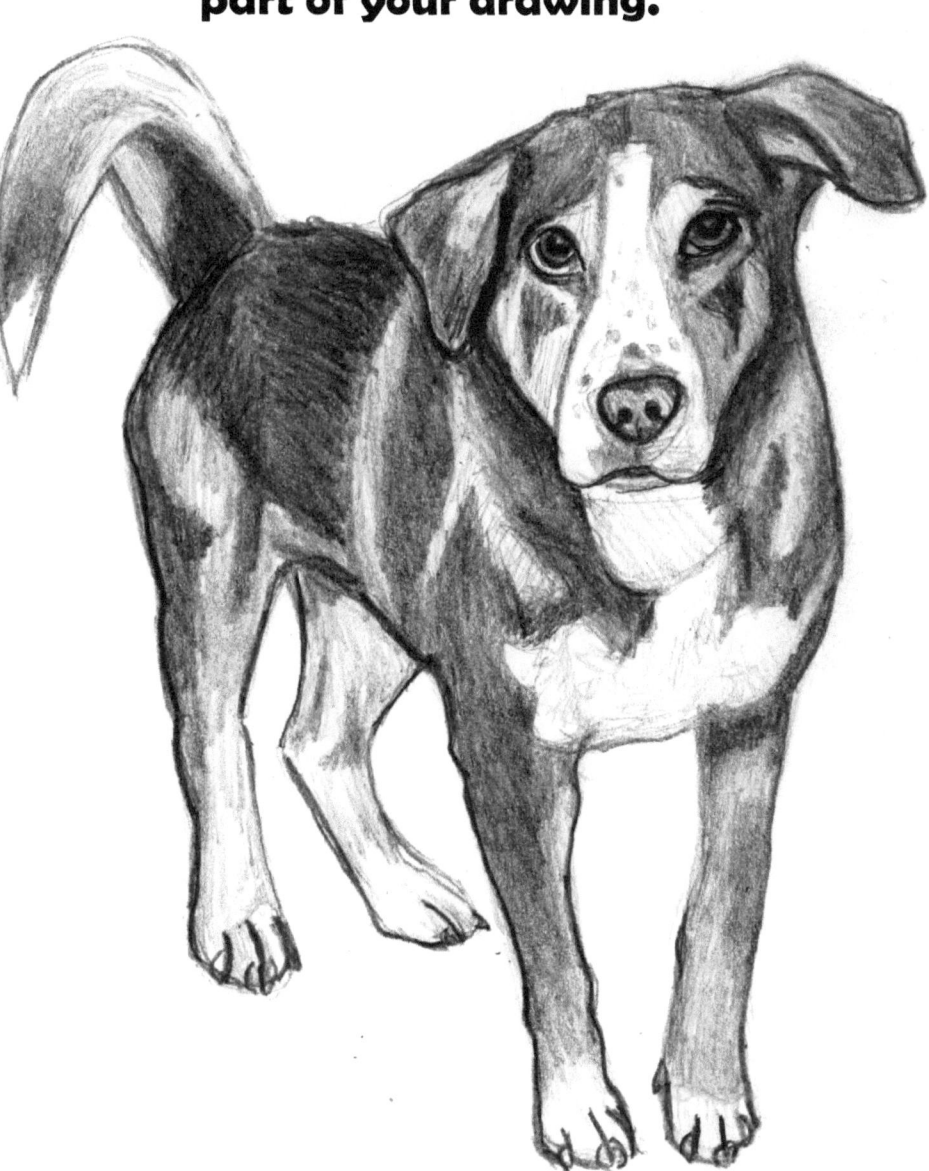

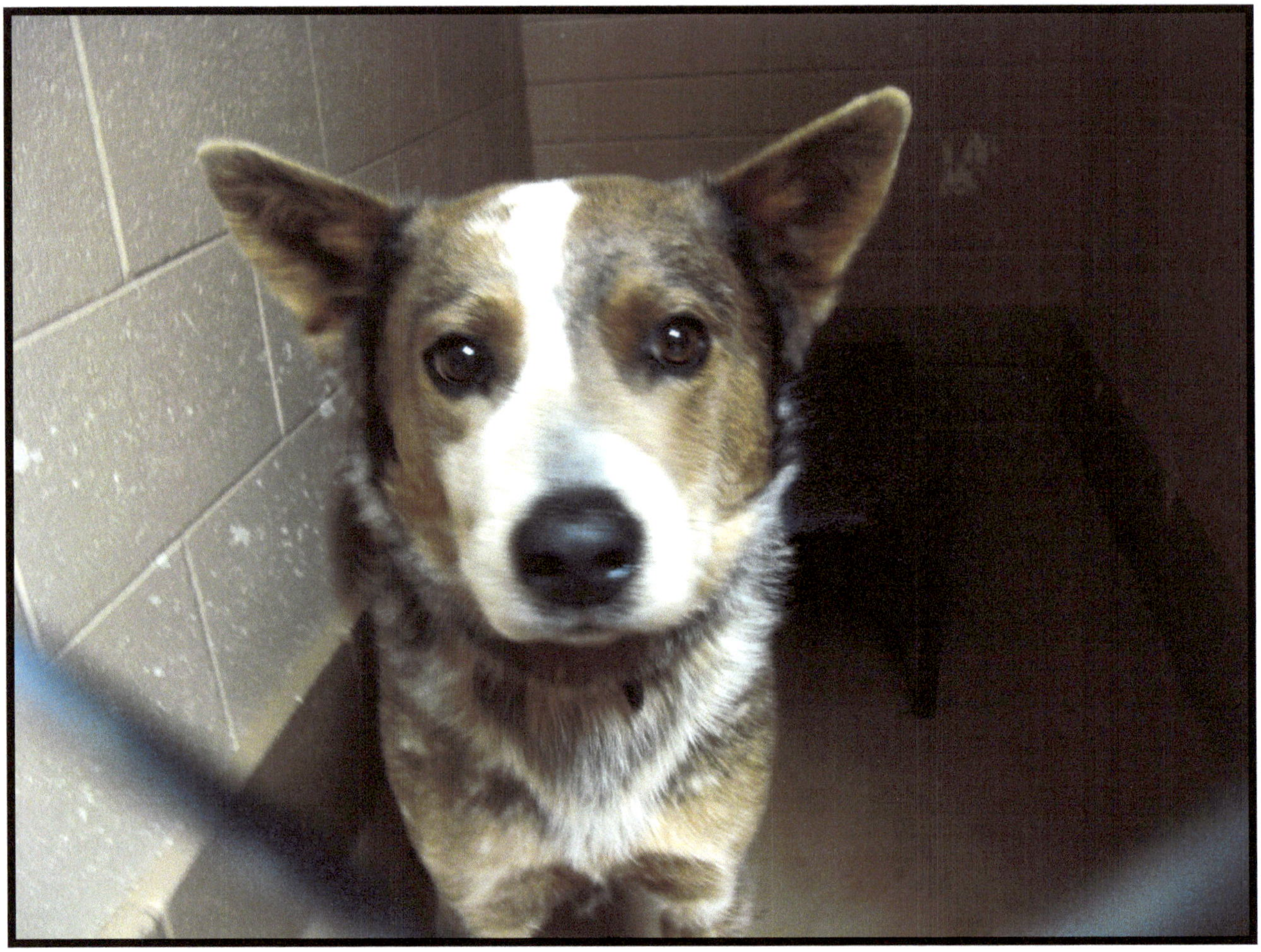

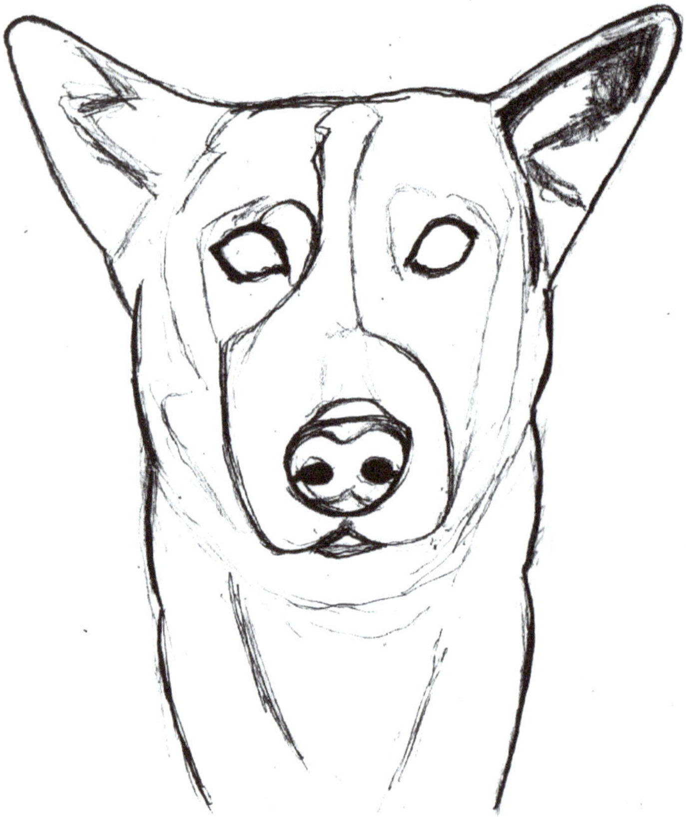

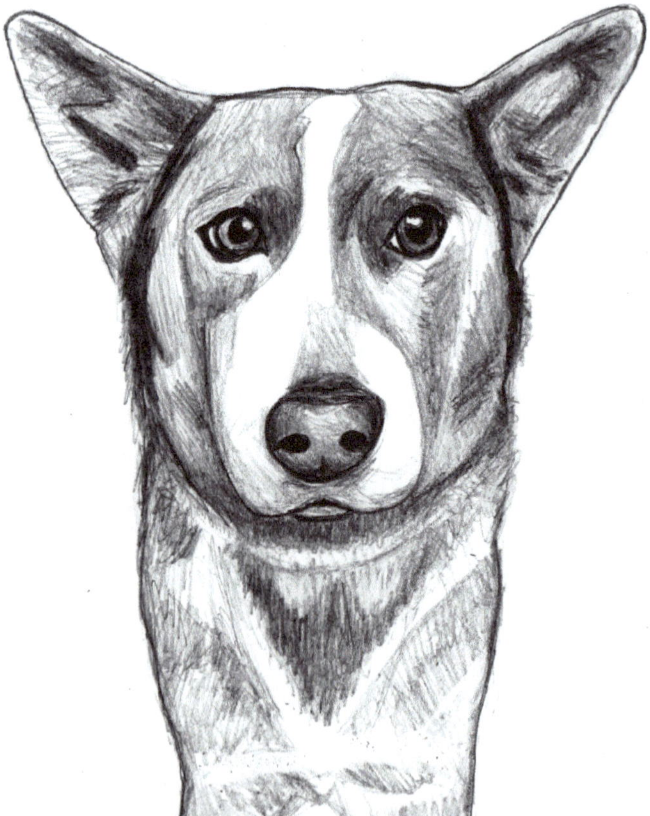

**Look forward to seeing these dogs and more in upcoming books written and illustrated by Kyle Jacob Adams**

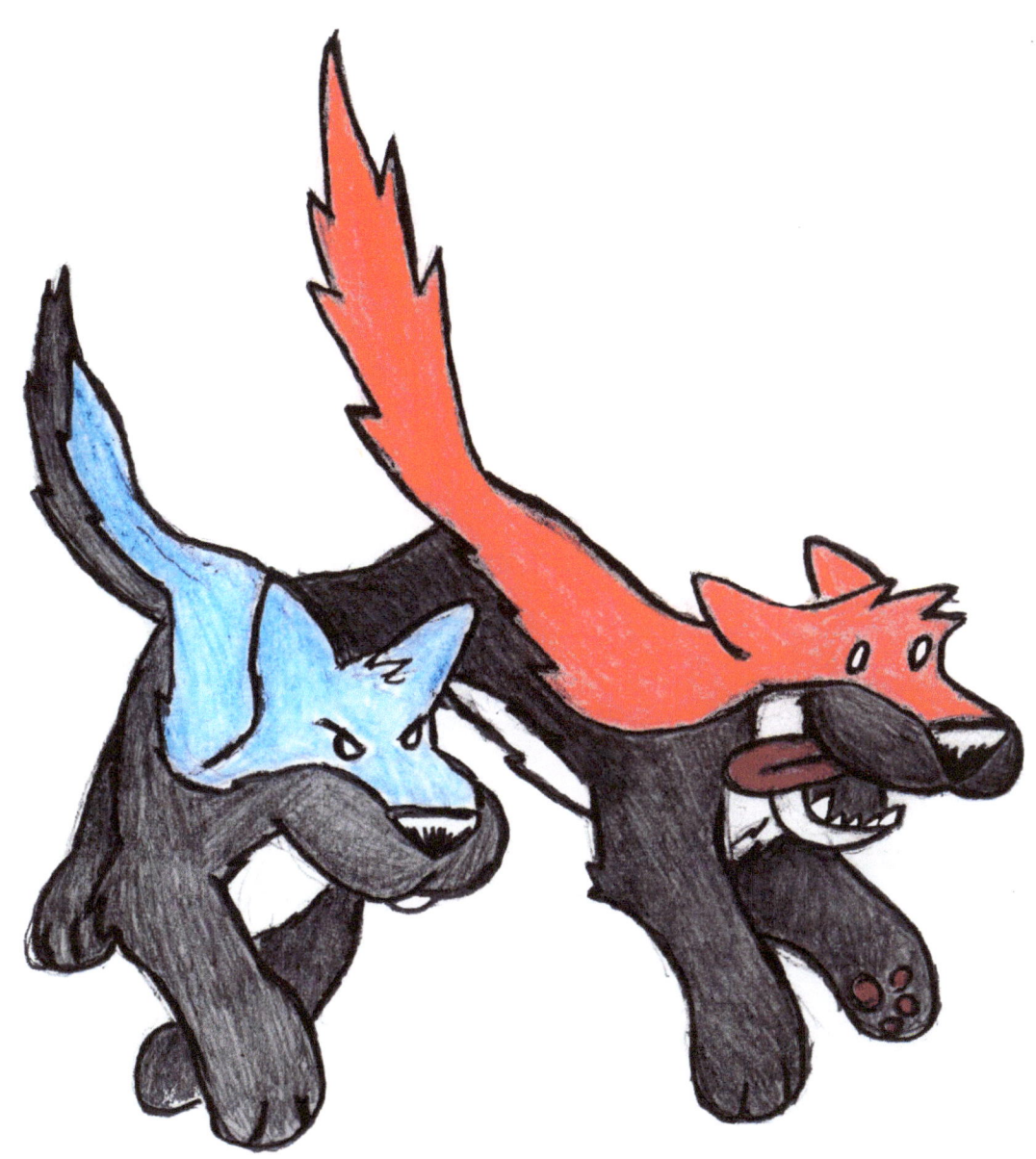

**Thank you for reading**

If this book has influenced you, or helped you grow in any way please leave a review at www.Amazon.com